PUBLIC LIFE
IN
BIBLE TIMES

PUBLIC LIFE
IN
BIBLE TIMES

Edited by

JAMES I. PACKER, A.M., D.PHIL.

Regent College

MERRILL C. TENNEY, A.M., Ph.D.

Wheaton Graduate School

WILLIAM WHITE, JR., Th.M., Ph.D.

THOMAS NELSON PUBLISHERS

Nashville • Camden • New York

621830

Published in Nashville, Tennessee, by Thomas Nelson, Inc., Publishers and distributed in Canada by Lawson Falle, Ltd., Cambridge, Ontario.

Printed in the United States of America.

Library of Congress Cataloging in Publication Data

Public life in Bible times.

  Includes index.
  1. Bible—Antiquities. 2. Palestine—Civilization. 3. Jews—Civilization.
I. Packer, J. I. (James Innell) II. Tenney, Merrill Chapin, 1904-
III. White, William, 1934-
BS621.P83 1985   220.9'5   85-5065
ISBN 0-8407-5984-3

INTRODUCTION

Public Life in Bible Times is based upon the latest findings of biblical, historical, and archaeological research regarding the public life and practices of the people of the Bible. Their customs, practices, and laws differed from ours quite sharply in some ways. In other ways they were nearer to us. In fact, many of our customs, practices, and laws derive at least in part from the ancient Hebrew people of Bible times.

Perhaps the most distinctive feature of public life in the Bible and a distinct way in which their life differed from ours was their practice of a theocratic form of government. God Himself was thought of as the ruling authority in the life of the nation. This concept colored all public life. From its very beginning as a nation, Israel was a religious community.

In the desert wanderings Moses spoke for God, but God Himself led Israel. Once in the land of Canaan, the Hebrew people looked upon their assigned property as a gift from God and believed they were obligated to practice faithful stewardship in their use of the land. Later the judges acted for God. The united kingdom under the authority of a central king came only when God's prophet found and anointed the person whom God himself had chosen for kingship. Partnership with God as a ruling authority acted as a controlling factor in all the life of Israel.

Even the economic life of the people was affected by this idea. God owned everything and ruled over all. Every person was expected to use his possessions as a sacred trust from God. *Public Life in Bible Times* is concerned with this idea and its place in the life of the nation of Israel. But it also discusses all aspects of public life: the development of government, transportation, money and economics, weapons and warfare, laws and statutes.

Public Life in Bible Times can be a guidebook to a greater understanding of the society of the biblical period. The Bible student should refer to it often for better understanding of God's eternal truth and how it can be applied to the world today.

TABLE OF CONTENTS

1

TRADE

People of the ancient Near East communicated mostly in person, and merchants of the day exchanged news and ideas along with their merchandise. For this reason, trade deeply affected society in Bible times; it opened the way for man's new discoveries about this world.

Traders took their caravans of camels and donkeys to the far reaches of the Near East, giving little thought to the time involved in the travel. Sometimes they spent a year or more in other countries, hawking their wares.

Sea captains often traded their services for part of the merchandise they carried. Sometimes there were no roads between cities of trade, so merchants had to take the high seas unless they simply cut across the desert.

Trade improved in peacetime. As nations formed alliances, their tradesmen shuttled to and fro, in spite of the dangers of traveling across foreign soil. Government leaders set up military posts; soldiers patrolled the roads; and courts took severe action against thieves on the road. Tradesmen in Bible times needed constant protecton from the danger of robbers.

But war meant trouble for tradesmen. The inflation rate soared; kings banned trade with some nations; and the roads were filled with armies instead of trade caravans. After war, the victors often imposed limits on the trade of conquered nations. This restricted their wealth and so prevented further rebellion.

Canaan was in a key trade position. The countries to her north (Phoenicia and Aram) and to the south (Egypt) used the public roads that ran through Canaan. She could not be isolated from her neighbors, even if she had wanted to be. This strategic location could have been used by Israel in order to proclaim God in her trade and cultural relations (Deut. 4:6). Instead, Israel became more and more like her ungodly neighbors, and she lost her distinctive quality of life as God's covenant people. God then allowed other nations to scatter the Israelites.

BEGINNINGS OF TRADE

The land determines what a nation can produce for trade. Climate, soil, raw materials, and the location of trade routes encourage or limit economic development.

Man needs food, and this is the most basic item of trade. In the earliest times, man collected wild grains and legumes and killed animals for meat. Because he constantly needed to search for food, he ignored most other needs. When man began running out of wild grain, he made a tough decision: He settled down and took the risk of trying to grow his own crops. He then faced the problems of lack of rain, locusts, untimely planting, wild animals, and floods. If his farming attempts failed, starvation would follow. When he decided to settle down, therefore, he had to consider such things as availability of water, fertility of the soil, and his ability to defend himself against hostile neighbors.

Man produced fruits and vegetables, dairy products, and meat products. He made tools and utensils with local raw materials. The producer traded with the consumer.

But as men formed larger communities and villages, their needs increased, and some of the settlers became tradesmen. They traded materials from several producers in their own villages for goods produced by neighboring villages. As these tradesmen moved about, they shared information about needs and supplies between one village and another, and soon particular communities began to specialize in certain kinds of work. One area produced wine, another dyed textiles, and so on. The merchant arranged trades between these communities.

Some areas started producing copper, bronze, iron, and other metals. Tradesmen had to go long distances to find these metals, and this is how distant trade began. Merchants took raw materials from the mines and delivered them to craftsmen, who made them into needed tools and finished products. Then the merchants took the tools to farmers, hunters, and others who needed them.

The desire for raw materials explains why the ancient nations needed good trade relations. It also explains why they engaged in war to control areas that produced these materials. Egypt, Mesopotamia, Anatolia, Syria, Phoenicia, and Canaan were connected by trade routes before 3000 B.C. In fact, archaeologists have found evidence of a network of Near Eastern trade routes that existed before 3000 B.C. Caravans moved from one end of the "Fertile Crescent" to the other—from the Persian Gulf to Asia Minor, Syria, Canaan, and Egypt.

Sea trade soon became common. The Phoenicians built a great fleet and used colonies along the coast of the Mediterranean as trading posts. The cities of Tyre and Sidon became trading centers

Goldworking. This relief in an Egyptian tomb at Sakkarah (*ca.* 2300 B.C.) shows scenes from the process of goldworking. In the upper left, gold is weighed on scales and a scribe records the weight. To the right, men blow through tubes to make the fire hot enough to melt the metal. In the lower section, craftsmen fashion gold objects on tables. The finished objects rest on a shelf in the center frame.

for many nations; they had good harbors and lay near the important land routes. Many ships stopped there to unload their goods.

Merchants depended on special privileges to do their work. When kings made treaties, they gave special status for some merchants; they were considered to be the official representatives of the nation. Because the kings protected them, they were called "king's merchants." Solomon imported horses through "king's merchants" (1 Kings 10:28). The king of Byblos wrote: "Aren't there 20 ships in my harbor which are in *commercial relations* with Ne-su-Ba-neb-Ded? As to Sidon,... aren't there 50 more ships there which are in *commercial relations* with Werket-El, and which are drawn up to his house?" (italics ours)[1]

The prosperity of a nation depended on its raw materials and its trade relations with other countries. This is why the various countries needed an extensive system of transportation. Early merchants exchanged one product for another, a transaction that we call a *barter*. Later they paid for goods with gold or silver. Nations agreed on a set value for these metals, and this value might change over the years.

Abraham paid 400 shekels of silver for the cave of Machpelah, for example, and Joseph's brothers sold him for 20 shekels of silver. By the sixth century B.C., merchants were using coins for payment. Most merchants used coins by the time of Jesus. Thus, Jesus could ask about the image that was on the face of a Roman coin (Luke 20:19-26).

A. Egypt. Egypt soon controlled the metal market in the Near East. The Egyptian pharaohs kept a tight rein on the mining of gold in their country. This metal was so scarce that it became precious, and among merchants it was the most prized form of payment. Egypt actually became a superpower because of her control of gold. The gold used for the burial of Tutankhamen ("King Tut") shows Egypt's riches, even in a time of lessening wealth.

Egypt was also rich in silver; Egyptian jewelers added it to gold as an alloy. About 3000 B.C., silver was valued more than gold, but merchants gradually came to value gold more. Thus, by 1500 B.C., gold was worth twice as much as silver; by 1000 B.C., the ratio of gold to silver was $3^1/_2$ to 1.

But Egypt's gold couldn't do everything. Egypt needed wood,

turquoise, and copper, and she had to trade to get them. The fancy life-style of her pharaohs strained Egypt's economy, and crop failure caused widespread famine.

First, therefore, Egypt had to make special trade deals to import the needed goods. Her earliest efforts brought trade contracts with Cyprus, Anatolia, Mesopotamia, and other Near East nations.

Egypt's next step was to colonize Syria and Palestine to safeguard the trade routes that brought in her raw materials. These routes brought foodstuffs and other vital supplies. Ships from Phoenicia brought timber for doors, paneling, coffins, and other special uses of the Egyptian royal family—including wood for the chambers of the tombs. Copper came by sea from Cyprus and Asia Minor.

Then Egypt explored the vast desert regions east of Egypt, especially Sinai and the southern Negev, searching for copper and turquoise. Egypt had much to offer the world, such as linens and papyrus (which was her most important contribution to Western civilization, in the long run). Papyrus (from which we get the word *paper*) was a sturdy writing material made from flax pulp, woven together with beaten strips of papyrus reed. Some papyrus manuscripts have lasted 4,500 years.

B. Canaan. Canaan has always been a very fertile and fruitful land. In his tomb inscriptions, Pharaoh Weni tells of his military campaigns in Canaan. He took cities and destroyed vineyards and orchards (around 2500 B.C.—about the time of Abraham). Pharaoh Sinuhe (about 1950 B.C.) tells of living in the Yarmuk Valley where figs, grapes, honey, olives, fruit, and barley were plentiful. He writes:

> *Bread was made for me as a daily*
> *fare; wine as daily provision,*
> *cooked meat and roast fowl, besides*
> *the wild beast of the desert...*
> *and milk in every (kind of) cooking.*[2]

Moses' description of the land agrees. He said it was a land "of wheat and barley, of vines and fig trees and pomegranates, and a land of olive trees and honey" (Deut. 8:8). The people of Palestine have cultivated these products from early times, and they still form the backbone of the diet in Israel. When Joshua led the invasion of Canaan, the Israelites kept right on farming the crops the Canaanites had raised. Note: " 'The LORD your God brings you into the land...to give you...vineyards and olive trees which you did not plant, and you shall eat and be satisfied' " (Deut. 6:10-11, NASB). Ever since, the farming pattern of the Holy Land has stayed about the same.

Schoolboys in ancient Israel learned their farm calendar as set out in a poem found at Gezer in 1908. Some schoolboy learning to write at about Solomon's time recorded this breakdown of the farmer's year:

1. *His two months are (olive) harvest,*
2. *His two months are planting (grain),*
3. *His two months are late planting,*
4. *His month is hoeing up of flax,*
5. *His month is harvest of barley,*
6. *His month is harvest and feasting,*
7. *His two months are vine-tending,*
8. *His month is summer fruit.*

In ancient Israel, September and October were a harvest time of olives, grain, and grapes. In November and December, farmers planted grains and vegetables. In January and February, they sowed grains and vegetables for a later crop. In March, April, and May they harvested flax, then barley, wheat, and vegetables. Israelite farmers celebrated the end of the harvest with a time of feasting and praise to God. The hot, dry summer months produced little, so the farmer used that time to care for his vines and orchards; some orchards gave him fruit in August.

Canaan was a favorite trading spot, since it lay exactly on the major trade routes between Egypt, Syria, Phoenicia, Babylon, and Assyria. Canaan supplied honey, olive oil, grain, wine, and spices. Also, the ancient world had a growing need for tar and petroleum, which Canaan produced in great quantities. Many nations traded for it. Egypt readily sent supplies of pottery, metals, frankincense, and ivory in exchange for petroleum products. Ezekiel writes, " 'Judah and the land of Israel, they were your traders; with the wheat of Minnith, cakes, honey, oil and balm they paid for your merchandise' " (Ezek. 27:17, NASB). By the way, when the Bible mentions "oil," it usually means olive oil for cooking.

Local trade followed supply and demand—what was needed most would cost the most. The siege of Samaria shows this. War made food prices go up for Samaria. Traders couldn't get in the cities, and farmers couldn't get out to harvest their crops. Soon the people were eating everything—a donkey's head sold for 80 pieces of silver; a tiny amount of common weed sold for 5 pieces of silver. Starvation isn't pretty. The siege victims were even eating babies (2 Kings 6:28).

When the siege lifted, prices came down as food became available. " 'Tomorrow about this time a measure of fine flour shall be sold for a shekel, and two measures of barley for a shekel, in the gate of Samaria' " (2 Kings 7:1, NASB).

In ancient times, merchants conducted most of their business at

Gezer calendar. The inscription on this soft piece of limestone was probably a school exercise, recorded by a young boy learning to write. The verse traces the calendar of a farmer's year. The stone was found at Gezer and probably dates from the ninth or tenth century B.C.

the city gate. The gate soon became important in matters of government as well. The elders of the city met at the gate to deal with community and legal matters (Amos 5:10). Strangers were either welcomed to the city or refused entry at the gate.

So merchants came to Jerusalem with their grain, wine, figs, grapes and other products to sell at the main gate. But problems arose when they tried to do this on the Sabbath. Nehemiah would not allow trade at the gate on the Sabbath; he stationed guards there to enforce the law (Neh. 13:15-21).

False weights and measures were another kind of problem in Old Testament trade. You shall have "just balances, just weights, a just ephah, and a just hin" (Lev. 19:36). The lack of honesty in daily life—shown in the trade problems—tells us of much deeper problems with Israel. Prophets pointed to sharp practices in business to show the sad religious state of Israel: "Hear this, you who trample the needy...saying, 'When will the new moon be over, So that we may buy grain, And the sabbath, that we may open the wheat market, To make the bushel smaller and the shekel bigger, And to cheat with dishonest scales' " (Amos 8:4-5, NASB). Some merchants tried to ruin their fellow citizens with sharp business

Hebrew ostrakon. This potsherd (*ca.* eighth century B.C.) was found at Tell Qasile. It is inscribed, "Gold from Ophir to Beth-horon—30 shekels." Costly papyrus was not normally used for everyday writing in antiquity. Instead, potsherds (Greek, *ostraka*) were inscribed in ink or engraved with a stylus.

Weights. In the interest of fair trade, vendors weighed the metal used as currency against standard stone weights. These weights were discovered on the hill of Ophel in Jerusalem; they date from the seventh or early sixth century B.C. One weight bears the value of two shekels, another of four shekels, and the largest is valued at 24 shekels.

deals. If a farmer had a bad harvest, he might need to borrow money to buy food and plant the next crop. If the next crop was just as bad, ungodly lenders might then take all his property and sell his family into slavery. Israel's prophets condemned these wheeler-dealers for their lack of pity or any sense of fairness. They attacked shrewd merchants who took advantage of poor people, widows, and orphans. Isaiah says God searched the streets of Israel for right living and found sin instead: "Thus He looked for justice, but behold, bloodshed; For righteousness, but behold, a cry of distress. Woe to those who add house to house and join field to field, Until there is no more room, So that you have to live alone in the midst of the land!" (Isa. 5:7-8, NASB). Amos says these ungodly merchants were anxious " 'to buy the helpless for money and the needy for a pair of sandals' " (8:6; 2:6-8).

Women engaged in business as well as men. The writer of Proverbs tells us that a "virtuous" woman had many skills. She could weave the materials she purchased in the market to make cloth (31:13, 19, 21-22) and she could sew clothes and belts (31:24). She profited from wise buying, hard work, and good trading (31:24). Often she used her profits to buy land (31:16). The writer of Proverbs says an ideal woman is hard-working, mentally sharp, and alert in her business dealings. She is not shy or housebound. She proudly bids and pays for the things she buys. She is "like merchant ships," bringing profit to the family (31:14).

Theocratic (direct divine) rule was supposed not only to help Israel rule itself, but to enable it to influence other nations as well.

But each time Israel began associating with strong nations, it suffered. Its strength lay in its religious commitment, but this commitment wavered. If Israel had allowed God to rule completely, other nations would not have overrun it. But Israel kept ignoring Him.

Now we will review Israel's economic development, starting with the period of the United Kingdom.

TRADE IN THE KINGDOM OF DAVID AND SOLOMON

King Saul united the 12 tribes of Israel into one strong nation. By the time David ruled (tenth century B.C.), Israel was an established power. By war and by treaty, David brought the neighboring nations to his side, and many of them paid great sums of money to keep peace with Israel. The Bible doesn't give a total of this money (2 Sam. 8:2, 6, 11-12), but it must have been very large.

For instance, David received from Zobah 700 horsemen, 20,000 foot soldiers, 1,000 chariots and horses (2 Sam. 8:4; 1 Chron. 18:4). From Syria he received shields of gold and bronze; from Hamath, articles of silver, gold, and bronze; from Ammon, a heavy gold crown (2 Sam. 12:30). Israel lived at peace and became richer under David's rule. The Bible tells us little about trade during this time, but we know Israel grew rich from the agreements she made with her neighbors. David probably traded with his friend Hiram of Tyre and the nation must have profited by this friendship. Both Tyre and Phoenicia traded with Israel, "...for the Zidonians and they of Tyre brought much cedar wood to David" (1 Chron. 22:4).

Solomon continued to receive payments from weaker nations to keep peace, as his father David had (1 Kings 4:21). Notice how well the king's table was spread with foreign items: "And Solomon's provision for one day was thirty kors of fine flour and sixty kors of meal, ten fat oxen, twenty pasture-fed oxen, a hundred sheep besides deer, gazelles, roebucks, and fattened fowl. For he had dominion over everything west of the River, from Tiphsah even to Gaza, over all the kings west of the River; and he had peace on all sides around about him" (1 Kings 4:22-24, NASB).

Governors taxed local products, and these taxes supplied the needs of the king's palace: "they brought presents, and served Solomon all the days of his life" (1 Kings 4:21; 10:15). Surrounding kings paid their taxes in food, gold, silver, barley, and even straw for the horses (cf. 1 Kings 4:28).

More income for Israel's treasury came from merchants who wanted favors and would pay to get them. These traders would give gold or whatever was required to get special treatment from the king; Arab traders brought merchandise with them for this purpose (1 Kings 10:15). Even the Queen of Sheba brought fine gifts when she visited Solomon, no doubt to get special treatment for her merchants (1 Kings 10:2).

Solomon imported materials for the temple from neighboring lands (1 Kings 9:15). From Tyre he got cedar, cypress, and gold (1 Kings 5:8; 9:11,14). In return, he gave Hiram of Tyre 20,000 kors of wheat and 20 kors of oil as an annual payment.

Solomon became an international dealer. His ships had Phoeni-

Barter in the Bible

Barter is the simple exchange of one item or service for another. In ancient times, a carpenter might build a house for a farmer, in return for some vegetables and grain; cattlemen might trade cattle for hay; and so on.

In Eastern countries today, a section of each city is still designated as the place where craftsmen, importers, farmers, and businessmen can meet to barter their goods and services. In times of national crisis, barter often takes the place of cash sales. People of the United States and other Western nations commonly used barter during the Great Depression of the 1930s.

The Bible mentions several interesting examples of barter. One involved trading cattle for bread during the famine described in Genesis 47:13-17; this example shows that barter was used when money was no longer worth anything. Another barter involved the Israelites' trading of wheat for cedar trees, in order to build Solomon's Temple (1 Kings 5:1-12); this shows that barter was used in prosperous times, when one people had something that another needed, and would trade for it. Yet another interesting barter was Hosea's exchange of grain and silver for a wife (Hos. 3:2); this incident shows that barter was one way that a groom could pay for a wife, whose absence from her father's household decreased the work force in the home. (See "Marriage and Divorce.") This "dowry" concept is still used in some African nations.

Materials or services could be used for barter, as when Jacob bound himself to Laban as a servant to gain Laban's daughter for his bride (Gen. 29:15-30). When Joseph was sold into slavery, his services as a slave were exchanged for money or trade goods (Gen. 37:23-28). God ordained that the tribe of Levi should live by bartering their services as priests for food and meat, which were brought to the temple for sacrifice (Num. 18:25-32).

cian sailors on them; he used Ezion-geber on the Gulf of Eilat as his own port (1 Kings 9:16ff.). The royal merchants brought him gold, almug trees, precious stones, ivory, silver, apes, peacocks, and horses (cf. 1 Kings 9:28; 10:11-12, 14, 22, 26).

Solomon bought horses and chariots from Egypt and Que, paying 600 shekels of silver for a chariot and 150 shekels for each horse. In turn he sold these to Anatolia and Aram (1 Kings 10:29).

TRADE IN THE DIVIDED KINGDOM

When Israel split into two kingdoms, the wealth of the nation fell. Phoenicia became the strong commercial force in Palestine; her seaports and harbors on the Mediterranean helped greatly. Ezion-geber never regained its place as a first-rate trading port, but the Arameans of the north quickly grew into a strong military power.

The Phoenicians took control of Near Eastern markets by developing sea routes to Egypt, Cyprus, Crete, Sicily, North Africa (Carthage), Italy, and Spain. Phoenician ships may have gone as far as Cornwall (England). From the Red Sea they traded with Africa, Arabia, and India.

The Phoenicians planted colonies of their own people in foreign lands, to control better the trade there. Trade was their strength; they never tried to gain power by making war. Phoenicians had a reputation for landing the best deal they could make. Other nations accepted this peaceful practice; they knew they had nothing to fear from the Phoenicians.

The northern kingdom of Israel tried to copy the Phoenicians. King Ahab sealed a friendship with Phoenicia when he married the daughter of Ethbaal of Sidon (better known as Jezebel). He adopted Baal worship and copied Phoenician forms of art and building construction. When King Sargon II conquered Israel, he boasted that he received large tribute from Menahem, the last king. Archaeologists have found pieces of ivory from Israel in Sargon's palace at Nimrud; the ivory carvings copied Phoenician artwork. Similar carvings have been found in Samaria, showing the great influence that Phoenicia had on the northern kingdom.

Ezekiel tells us much about the Phoenicians' trading ways. He foretold that Babylon would take over the riches and power of Tyre, a Phoenician seaport. No longer could people say that Tyre is "of perfect beauty" (Ezek. 27:3), for she "never shalt be any more" (27:36). Ezekiel lists commodities that the Phoenicians traded. They sought trading opportunities as they sailed the Mediterranean and Red Seas (1 Kings 9:26-28; 2 Chron. 8:17-18). The Phoenicians were proud of their wealth, but Ezekiel predicted that they would crumble.

After the Phoenicians, the Aramaeans gained the upper hand in trading strength. They opened trading stalls in Samaria during Ahab's reign. As their armies conquered neighboring territory, they opened more markets and the Aramaean kingdom grew stronger. Then Ahab overthrew King Ben-hadad of Aram, and the two men signed a treaty that allowed the northern kingdom to open trading posts in Damascus (cf. 1 Kings 20:34).

Solomon's successors tried to use Ezion-geber as a trade port. They did not succeed because they had no political clout with the surrounding nations. Ezion-geber was Judah's southernmost city, about 200 miles below Jerusalem, and Judah could use it as a port only if she controlled the land of Edom. After Solomon's death, Edom grew strong and became a great trading power in its own right; the Edomites made good use of their key location at a crossing point in trade routes between Egypt and the Arabian Desert. But when Judah tried to use the port of Ezion-geber, the Edomites forced them out.

Because King Jehoshaphat wanted to build up the trading power of the south, he made a trading agreement with Ahab in the north. His successor, Ahaziah, tried to build ships at Ezion-geber and launch massive trading ventures for Jehoshaphat. But the ships never sailed; they were destroyed in the harbor (2 Chron. 20:37). That was the end of Judah's attempts at wide trade, even though King Uzziah of Judah brought Ezion-geber back under Judah's control a hundred years later (2 Chron. 26:2). Uzziah had a great interest in Judah's business welfare. He strengthened vital cities, built additional military outposts, and expanded Judah's farming area. We believe he strengthened Judah's trading ties with other nations and may have planned a large fleet of merchant ships.

But Babylon defeated Judah, and her trading friends jeered at

Bronze horse's bit. This bit comes from Palestine. Notice its circular cheek pieces, to which sharp spikes are fastened. It may date to the seventeenth century B.C.

her misfortune (Ezek. 25:32). After the Exile, God improved the trading efforts of His people as Persia, Greece, Egypt, Syria, and Rome struggled for control of Palestine; but the big trading days were over. In Jesus' time the Jews were mainly farmers and shepherds. Their Roman masters encouraged this, so that Palestine became the Roman Empire's "bread basket."

OBJECTS OF TRADE

What items were traded in the Near East through these years? Ezekiel listed some of the items (Ezek. 27). He tells not only what was traded, but where it came from. He lists raw materials such as cloth goods, precious stones, animals, farming products, carpets, cords, and even clothing. Animals and farm products were discussed in the section on Canaan; but let us look at the other goods in trade:

A. Gold. In Egypt, the Pharaoh's government owned all of the gold. Egypt's eastern desert was rich in gold ore and the kings mined it for their own treasuries. They used gold for decorations in the palace and various temples. The Egyptians used every method they could to get the gold; washing sand and gravel, combing the beaches for nuggets tossed up by the sea, and mining the underground deposits with slave labor. They could mine silver along with the gold, since it was often found in the same places. The ancients called the alloy of gold and silver *electrum*.

Israel had no gold in her land. The Israelites could see tiny particles of gold in the quartzite and granite of the Eilat Mountains, but it was never worth mining. When Moses led the Israelites out of Egypt, the Egyptians gave them gifts of gold, just to get rid of these people who brought the plagues (Exod. 12:35). The Israelites used much of this gold to decorate the ark of the covenant and the tabernacle (Exod. 35:5). They wasted some of the same gold in making the golden calf (Exod. 32:3-4). As Joshua swept through Canaan, he collected a great deal of gold and other booty, but it was lost in later years when other conquerers defeated Israel.

David gathered gold by demanding taxes or tribute from nations he had defeated in battle, and from nations that were weak and fearful of Israel's army (2 Sam. 8:10; 12:30; 1 Chron. 18:10). David himself gave 100,000 talents of gold for the temple construction (1 Chron. 22:14), while the other leaders of Israel gave 5,000 talents and 10,000 darics of gold (1 Chron. 29:7, RSV).

As Israel flexed her military muscles, other nations paid tribute in gold and silver (1 Kings 9:14; 10:14ff.). For example, the Queen of Sheba gave lavish donations to the high-living court of Solomon: "And she gave the king a hundred and twenty talents of gold, and a very great amount of spices and precious stones. Never again did such abundance of spices come in as that which the queen of Sheba gave King Solomon" (1 Kings 10:10, NASB).

Then Israel's state changed, and her neighbors demanded peace payment in gold and other precious metals, often in huge amounts (1 Kings 14:26; 15:18ff.; 23:33; 25:15).

The value of gold was great, yet the Israelites did not use it for money, but mainly for decorations. Since gold is a soft metal, craftsmen could shape it in a variety of ways for elaborate objects. The Bible mentions fancy cups and bowls, especially for royal use (Esther 1:17); gold-leaf decorations on the tabernacle, the throne, and the walls of the palace; golden objects used in worship in the temple; and jewelry for women (Gen. 24:22; Num. 31:50).

B. Silver. People used silver for money in these early times. Traders recognized a set value for a given amount of silver. The Egyptians and early Sumerians got silver from northern Syria and parts of Egypt; as we have already noted, the Egyptian mines often produced a combination of gold and silver.

Silver became an important factor in trading in the ancient world. Conquered nations used it to pay tribute (1 Kings 9:14). Worshipers brought it as a gift to the temple in Jerusalem (1 Chron. 29:4). The modern Hebrew word for silver has extended its most common meaning to signify "money."

C. Copper. Copper and bronze are ancient products of Canaan. Looking back, we find that the Canaanites learned the art of *smelting* (heating ore to melt the metal and separate it from the rock) as early as 3500 B.C. The Arabah produced malachite, an ore that was high in copper content, and the people of that region mined it extensively. They built a copper-smelting factory at Tel Abu Matar, southwest of Beer-sheba, in about 3500 B.C. Arab craftsmen sent expeditions into the Sinai Desert to get their copper (about 3000 B.C.).

Archaeologists once thought King Solomon opened the mines at Timna and a smelting plant at Ezion-geber. Nelson Glueck discovered these sites. But more recent researchers have found that the mines were Egyptian, and date from about 1300 to 1150 B.C. We know this because the Timna mines were dedicated to an Egyptian goddess, Hathor. Diggers have unearthed a temple there with inscriptions in the Egyptian language.

Solomon used huge quantities of copper in building the temple at Jerusalem (1 Chron. 18:8), and explorers have tried to find where it all came from. They found evidence at Ezion-geber of what they thought were Solomon's copper mines; turned out to be a spot where caravans of traders stopped to rest. Most likely the copper came from the Arabah desert at Punon, a spot the Israelite caravans passed on their way across Jordan (Num. 33:42ff.). Israeli archaeologists discovered large-scale copper mines at Timna in the Sinai that date back to Egyptian times. These mines are now being exploited by modern mining techniques.

Egypt's business leaders combed the Sinai for copper; they used copper mines at Serabit-el-Khadem beside the Gulf of Suez and in the southern Negev near Ezion-geber, on the Gulf of Eilat. But most of the Egyptian copper came from the island of Cyprus; in fact, our English word *copper* comes from the name of that island. Copper drew Cyprus into the trading plans of many nations—especially Greece, Asia Minor, and Syria. Between 2000 and 1000 B.C., Cyprus arose as a major trader in the Mediterranean world.

Researchers have found a letter from a ruler of Cyprus, agreeing to barter copper for famous Egyptian chariots and beds. It reads: "And have I not sent to thee through my messengers one hundred talents of copper? Furthermore, now, let thy messenger bring, for presents, one bedstead of ebony, inlaid with gold, and a chariot, with gold...and two horses."

So the discovery and use of copper prospered the trading world of the Near East. Copper had many more uses than silver or gold; its hardness made it ideal for many practical uses. And it was easier to find.

But many countries had no copper of their own. In Israel, for example, David needed more copper than the land could provide. So he accepted bronze (an alloy of copper and tin) as part of the tribute he demanded from Hadadezer of Aram (1 Chron. 18:8). David stored large quantities of copper for building the temple. Also, the king of Hamath sent bronze to David (1 Chron. 18:10). Armies used copper for helmets, swords, mace heads, and other weapons. Religious objects were made of copper—pans, wands, idols. Kitchen utensils were made of copper; women used it for mirrors and powder boxes; and most musical instruments were made of copper.

Archaeologists found that a spot called "the Cave of the Treasure," near the temple at En-gedi, held a large store of copper ob-

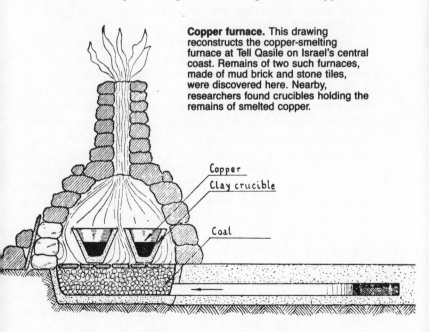

Copper furnace. This drawing reconstructs the copper-smelting furnace at Tell Qasile on Israel's central coast. Remains of two such furnaces, made of mud brick and stone tiles, were discovered here. Nearby, researchers found crucibles holding the remains of smelted copper.

Copper
Clay crucible

Coal

jects. Priests from the temple stored 429 prized objects there, wrapped in straw mats (about 3000 B.C.). Of these, many were copper: 10 crowns, 80 wands and 240 mace heads.

D. Tin. People of the ancient world needed tin to make bronze. By combining copper and tin, they could produce a stronger, tougher metal. The Phoenicians sold tin, but we're not sure where they found it. Perhaps it came from Cornwall in England, which was rich in tin.

E. Iron. In early centuries, man learned how to take iron from iron ore. But the real surge towards an iron industry came when man discovered the ore could be heated to melt the iron away from the rock. This iron industry began in Asia Minor around 1400 B.C. In Egypt and parts of Asia, ironworkers built special iron furnaces that used very hot air blasts to melt the ore and produce liquid iron, that then could be cast into molds. Our Bible tells us that Moses and the Israelites knew of this process: " 'But the LORD has taken you out and brought you out of the iron furnace, from Egypt, to be a people for His own possession, as today' " (Deut. 4:20, NASB). " 'And I will also break down your pride of power; I will also make your sky like iron and your earth like bronze' " (Lev. 26:19, NASB).

The Israelites depended on the power of the Lord to defeat the Canaanites. We realize this even more when we look at the kinds of weapons they had. The Israelites were poorly equipped for war, for the Canaanites had "chariots of iron." In Judges we read: "Now the LORD was with Judah, and they took possession of the hill country; but they could not drive out the inhabitants of the valley because they had iron chariots" (Judg. 1:19, NASB).

Later, when Israel was weak, the Philistines threatened them. As the Philistines moved into the southwestern shore of Canaan (about 1200 B.C.), they brought the skills of casting iron tools and weapons—skills they had learned from the Hittites in Asia Minor. Soon the Israelites began to buy iron farming tools from the Philistines instead of developing their own iron industry. The Philistines tried to keep it that way: "Now no blacksmith could be found in all the land of Israel, for the Philistines said, 'Lest the Hebrews make swords and spears.' So all Israel went down to the Philistines, each to sharpen his plowshare, his mattock, his axe, and his hoe. And the charge was two-thirds of a shekel for the plowshares, the mattocks, the forks, and the axes, and to fix the hoes. So it came about on the day of the battle that neither sword nor spear was found in the hands of any of the people who were with Saul or Jonathan, but they were found with Saul and his son Jonathan" (1 Sam. 13:19-22, NASB).

David made sure his people got their fair share of the iron. As he extended the borders of Israel, more of this raw material became available.

David got as much iron as he needed for weapons and other military needs; and he got ready for building the temple by storing up great quantities of iron. The Bible says, "David prepared large quantities of iron to make the nails for the doors of the gates and for the clamps, and more bronze than could be weighed" (1 Chron. 22:3, NASB).

As David's armies won in battle, they brought back iron implements as part of their loot. The soldiers gave 100,000 talents of iron to help in building the temple (1 Chron. 29:7). Archaeologists realized how valuable iron was at that time when they discovered a stockpile of iron bars weighing a total of 330,000 pounds in the palace of Sargon II who lived in Nineveh about 715 B.C. Surely King David forced the nations around him to give such iron bars to Israel as part of their peace tribute.

The Israelites never practiced iron smelting, as far as we know. Even though the Hermon Mountains in Carmel and the Arabah held plenty of iron ore, Israel depended on iron imports from Syria, Cyprus, and Asia Minor.

Iron was in great demand. It was harder and more plentiful than copper, so merchants all over the Near East traded with it. Armies used iron for daggers, shields, spearheads, and arrowheads. Farmers wanted iron for hoes, plowshares, picks, and sickles.

F. Ivory. Because ivory comes from the tusks of elephants, it was hard to get in the Near East. Rich families wanted it for jewelry and decorative furniture. Elephants once lived in Syria, but the search for ivory killed off all of them by 800 B.C. Most ivory used in the Near East came from the so-called Asiatic elephants.

Craftsmen around Beer-sheba made ivory figurines as early as 3500 B.C. Diggings in the Near East have turned up many ivory carvings, like those at Ugarit in Syria (dated about 1300 B.C.). At Megiddo archaeologists found 200 pieces of finely carved ivory below the palace of the governor; they date from about 1150 B.C.

Solomon's merchant ships brought him ivory for his throne (1 Kings 10:18-22). Ahab ordered his craftsmen to build an "ivory house," because he so admired the fine ivory work done by the Phoenicians (1 Kings 22:39). Pieces of ivory were inlaid in the walls of this house, and it contained many hand-carved ivory figurines. These included figures of people, animals, flowers, plants, and mythological figures.

Ancient sculptures used ivory to make chairs, couches, beds, boxes, and caskets. Soon the rich people of Samaria wanted these ivory creations. Because they'd gotten their riches by mistreating the people, Amos foretold that the rich Samaritan houses of ivory would be destroyed (3:15). The Assyrians made his forecast come true when they captured Samaria in 722 B.C. They looted the palaces of Samaria and took the ivory to Sargon II. Recent diggings show that the palace of Sargon II at Nimrud had ivory carvings much like the ones found in Samaria.

When Assyrians forced the southern kingdom to pay tribute, it included gifts of ivory. The Assyrian records say: "Hezekiah...did send me later to Nineveh...30 talents of gold, 800 talents of silver, precious stones, antimony, large cuts of red stone, couches (inlaid) with ivory, nimedu chairs (inlaid) with ivory...." (Pritchard, p. 201).

G. Glass. Because it was so rare, glass was a form of wealth; Job tells us " 'gold or glass cannot equal it (wisdom): nor can it be exchanged for articles of fine gold' " (Job 28:17, NASB). Before craftsmen developed the art of glass blowing, they molded the glass around an inner core while the glass was in a sticky, plastic form. When the glass cooled and hardened, they took away the core and the glass object was ready for use. Artisans used this process widely in Egypt and Mesopotamia about 2500 B.C. Archaeologists have discovered a glass factory that operated at El-Amarna in Egypt about 1400 B.C.; it produced small glass bottles that were exported to Palestine. The Egyptians also sent these bottles to Hara, Cyprus, and the Aegean Islands. The Mesopotamians did not export their glass objects as far away as Palestine. The Phoenicians made glass vessels to resemble alabaster; the Egyptians were also good at making glass pots, bottles, and other vessels, and coloring them to look like the original containers.

The Phoenicians began making blown glass about 100 B.C. They could produce blown glass much more rapidly than molded glass, so this lowered the cost of glass objects and made them more common. Romans used these glass vessels nearly as much as pottery. You will remember that a woman anointed Jesus with ointment from a glass bottle (Matt. 26:7).

H. Wood. Wood is one of man's oldest working materials. People of the Near East developed many uses of wood, and the area still depends heavily on wood today. Carpenters and wood craftsmen made furniture, tools, and idols (Deut. 4:28). They used it for paneling rooms, building homes, strengthening forts, and constructing ships. When woodsmen cleared hills near villages, the rains caused the bare soil to erode. This made much of the rocky, bare landscape of Israel today. Now the Near East has virtually no forests, though fine forests stood there in early centuries.

When the Israelites invaded Canaan, they took the hill country first and left the Canaanites in the valleys. On the hills, the Israelites steadily cut down all the trees for homes and for making farm tools. They also used the wood for fuel.

Solomon wanted fine cedar lumber for the temple, and he had to get it from Phoenicia. For 25 years workmen cut timber and shipped it to Solomon, landing at the port of Joppa (2 Chron. 2:16). Solomon also ordered fir and almug trees for building his palace.

The area of Bashan had fine oak forests; Israelite craftsmen made oars and furniture from oak. The Phoenicians exported much of the oak wood from Bashan to distant ports of the Mediterranean, even as far as Egypt.

Egypt lacked wood, so the pharaohs sent merchant fleets out to countries like Lebanon to get wood for their fine palaces and temples.

I. Bitumen. The word *pitch* in the Bible refers to bitumen, a thick form of oil. Bitumen seeps to the surface of the earth from deep layers of rock. It is much like asphalt. We find large quantities of bitumen floating on the surface of the Asphalt Lake on the island of Trinidad, and near the Dead Sea. Genesis 14:20 says that the kings of Sodom and Gomorrah fell into bitumen pits by the Dead Sea, and Noah waterproofed the ark by coating it with bitumen (Gen 6:14).

J. Flax. Egypt produced fine linens from the flax plants that grew so well along the Nile Valley. The Egyptians had a secret way of softening the flax fibers to make the linen more comfortable to wear; this made their products more popular. They placed the stalks of flax into water until they started to rot; then they dried the stalks and beat them to separate the fibers. Expert weavers spun the fibers into thread and wove it to make cloth.

The Egyptians used linen to wrap the embalmed bodies of the dead. They usually left the linen at its natural color, but they dyed some linen a red color to be used by the royal family. The Egyptians gave their word for linen *(sas)* to the Hebrew language.

The Israelites grew flax near Jericho and in the area of Galilee. They used dew water instead of running water to soften the stalks; this was easier, but it didn't give their linen the fine quality that Egyptian linen had. The Israelites learned the art of weaving from the Egyptians and the Bible often mentions how they used this skill. Sinai women made linens for the tabernacle (Exod. 35:25); priests and kings wore linen clothes (Exod. 28:39; 39:27-29; 1 Sam. 2:18; 2 Sam. 6:14; 1 Chron. 15:27-28). An angel who appeared to Daniel was dressed in linen (Dan. 10:5). Rich men like Mordecai wore linen (Esther 18:15); the rich man who spoke to Lazarus was dressed in fine linen (Luke 16:19). And remember that the body of Jesus was wrapped in linen for burial (Luke 23:53).

K. Cotton. Cotton was the poor man's cloth; it was more plentiful than linen and more widely used. Cotton came directly from the cotton plants of the field, and it needed far less processing to make it usable. Farmers raised the best quality cotton in the humid climate of Upper Egypt. Most often the Egyptians used cotton in its natural color, rather than dyed.

L. Wool. Wool comes from sheep, which were abundant and common in the ancient world. The people of the Near East raised sheep and goats from very early times, and they commonly wore clothing of wool. The weavers and dyers of the Near East developed cloth-making into a fine craft. Many villages became famous for their weaving and dyeing industries; for example, archaeologists have found a famous dyeing workshop at Tell Beit Mirsim.

2

TRANSPORTATION

The land in which Jesus walked and taught is small—just a narrow strip of land east of the Mediterranean Sea. But the nations around Israel were often passing through it and needed its strategic location and they often fought over it. Egypt, Assyria, Babylon, Persia, Greece, and Rome all wanted to control that special territory.

The world of the Near East is full of barriers—seas, rivers, deserts, and mountains. These barriers were vital to Israel's defense. For example, enemy armies were often stopped by mountains; they could go over them only if they found a natural pass. So Israel built fortified cities to guard these natural passes and routes of travel. Settled people could live at the edge of a desert, but this was often dangerous. Nomads from the desert would invade these villages when food was scarce; they might invade them at other times simply to rob and steal. People could cross rivers by fords or by walking across shallow spots. They could sail the seas in ships. Thus, geographical barriers did not stop those who wished to cross them.

In the Near East no nation had everything it needed for daily life; each depended on others for some of its needs. Both raw materials and finished products had to be traded. Ships traveled between ports of trading nations.

ROAD SYSTEMS OUTSIDE PALESTINE

The nations surrounding Palestine used their roads for commerce and communication, as well as for military routes in times of war. Even before the Roman Empire brought its famous road system to the Near East, this area had developed effective routes for long-distance transportation.

A. Asia Minor. Asia Minor is a flat plain about 900 to 1500 m. (3,000 to 5,000 ft.) in altitude bordered by mountains on the south ranging up to 4,000 m. (13,000 ft.). Asia Minor has water on three of its sides: the Mediterranean Sea to the south, the Aegean Sea to the west, and the Black Sea to the north. Steep, rocky mountains rim the coast of the Black Sea, forming a natural barrier to roads linking the northern and southern territories of Asia Minor. The ancient Lydians settled in the fertile valleys of western Asia Minor along the Aegean Sea. In this area Croesus, the last king of Lydia (an ancient country of Asia Minor), was defeated in battle by the Persians. The Taurus Mountains in the south were a serious barrier to people wanting to come north from the Mediterranean Sea. But these travelers could follow gorges through the mountains. Paul used one of these passes—known as the Cilician Gates—on his second and third journeys through Derbe, Lystra, Iconium, and Antioch (Acts 15:41; 16:1; 18:23ff.). The central plateau of Asia Minor is made up of rolling hills, basins, marshes, and volcanic cones. The mountains that hem it in limit the amount of rainfall. Its bare terrain is used by shepherds and their flocks.

The strength of Asia Minor in the ancient world lay in its mineral resources. Silver and copper were mined in Cappadocia, north of the Taurus Mountains. The Pontus region included the Hittite capital of Hattushash, which was a center for wood, silver, copper, and iron. Lead was mined near the Hellespont in northwest Asia Minor.

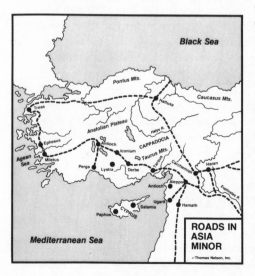

B. Cyprus. Cyprus was an island in the Mediterranean Sea, just 72 km. (45 mi.) south of Asia Minor and 96 km. (60

mi.) west of Syria. Its shape was much like a deerskin with its "tail" pointed toward Syria. It was 222 km. (138 mi.) long and 96 km. (60 mi.) wide at its widest point. The terrain resembled Asia Minor—mountains to the north (the Kyrenia Range) and the south, with the Mesaoria Plateau lying between. The plateau produced grain and the mountains yielded timber, copper, silver and possibly iron. Cyprus' wealth of natural products, its natural harbors (Salamis and Paphos), and its convenient position along Mediterranean trade routes made it a busy trading area in the earliest times. Acts 13:5 tells of Paul's arrival at Salamis by ship. He traveled by road from Salamis to Paphos, sharing the gospel of Christ as he went. At Paphos he rebuked a magician named Barjesus or Elymas. The governor heard Paul's preaching of the gospel, and believed in Jesus (Acts 13:12). Paul left Cyprus for Asia Minor, sailing from the port of Paphos (13:13).

C. Syria (Aram). The area along the eastern end of the Mediterranean Sea—from the Taurus Mountains in the north to the Sinai Desert in the south—encompassed several different kinds of geography and climate. The Egyptians named the region *Retenu*, "the land of the Asiatics." Its only unifying feature was the Rift Valley, running from the Amanus Mountains to the Gulf of Eilat.

The Orontes River drained the northern part of the Rift Valley, including part of the Beqa Valley. The Litani River drained between the Heman Mountains and Lebanon. The Jordan drained rainfall from the southern Beqa and the Hula Valley into the Dead Sea. The Aravah Valley ran southward from the Dead Sea to the Gulf of Eilat.

Today's Syria includes

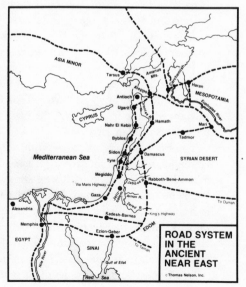

ROAD SYSTEM
IN THE
ANCIENT
NEAR EAST

© Thomas Nelson, Inc.

the area of ancient Phoenicia and Aramaea. The Aramaeans were seldom united. For example, we read about the rival Aramaean tribes of Aram-Zobah (2 Sam. 8:3ff.; 10:6, 8), Aram-Damascus, Arpad, and Hamath. The Phoenicians controlled the coastal harbors (except for Ugarit) all the way to the Amanus Mountains; but Syria controlled the roads from Asia Minor to Mesopotamia, Palestine, Egypt, and the Syrian Desert. Syria's western border, comprised primarily by the Amanus Mountain range, touched Phoenicia's coastal plains. The Orontes and the Khabur Rivers broke up this mountain range on their way to the Mediterranean. The valleys of these rivers were swamplands, where malaria posed a continual health problem.

The Anti-Lebanon Mountains formed the western border of Syria. These mountains rose up quickly out of the Beqa Valley; their layers of rock soaked up rainwater and drained it into a number of streams in the Syrian Desert. Damascus received its water from the southern slopes of the Anti-Lebanon Mountains, which made the city a desert oasis. As the capital of the Aramean kingdom, Damascus was of great importance in the Near East.

Damascus lay at the crossing point of international trade routes: the desert route from Babylon by way of Mari and Damascus, the Beqa road from northern Mesopotamia to Asia Minor by way of Aleppo and Hamath, the inland route of the *Via Maris* from Egypt to Mesopotamia, and the King's Highway from Ezion-geber to Amman. All went by way of Damascus.

Trade caravans met at Damascus, and this became a key factor in the city's prosperity. Merchants of the area sold oil and wine to the passing caravans and bartered for their goods. The caravans exchanged news from all over the Near East as traders mingled in the streets of Damascus.

The Book of Acts tells how Saul, a follower of the Jewish rabbi Gamaliel, was traveling from Jerusalem to Damascus to rout out followers of Jesus who had been strengthening the church there. While he was on that road, Jesus spoke to Saul and convinced him to stop persecuting the Christians. Acts 9:17-22 tells of Saul in Damascus, where he became a firm believer in Christ. He left that city to spend three years in the desert before returning to Damascus and then to Jerusalem, where he met Peter (Gal. 1:16-18).

D. Phoenicia. The peoples of Canaan who lived along the coast were called *Phoenicians*; they earned their living in shipping and came to be great sailors. Their land was enclosed by the Mediterranean Sea on the west and two sets of mountains on the east: the Amanus and the Lebanon Mountains. The people of Phoenicia expanded by trade and by sending people to colonize other lands.

Water from the rains and snows in the highlands sank into the layers of rock in the mountains and came back out at lower levels as springs and rivers. This supply of water allowed the people of the coastal area to farm the slopes. Villages grew up on the mountainsides.

The Beqa Valley between the Lebanon Range and the Anti-Lebanon was up to 16 km. (10 mi.) wide and 161 km. (100 mi.) long. It had a deep, rich soil south of Baalbek, between the Orontes and Litani Rivers. The Litani River ran for 112 km. (70 mi.) through the Beqa and turned for its last 32 km. (20 mi.) westward through gorges in the Lebanon Range to reach the Mediterranean. A road connected the seaports of Ugarit, Byblos, Sidon, and Tyre along the Mediterranean; but it never developed into a major highway because of the easier connections by way of the sea. To make road travel worse, each of these cities charged a toll for use of the road near their city; such tolls would not be charged when traveling by sea. Sidon and Tyre were directly connected by road with Canaan; this road was called *Via Maris* or "Way of the Sea." These cities exercised a great influence on the more primitive cities of Canaan.

ROAD SYSTEM IN PALESTINE

The first roads were sheep or cattle trails—dirt paths. Some roads followed *wadis*, dry river beds that carried water only in heavy rain seasons. Some roads were built through mountain passes. As trade grew, it became more important to get to and from neighboring countries by road. Nations bartered their own natural products, their ores or minerals. Many merchants had to pass through Palestine, because Palestine lay on the natural route from Egypt to the southwest, Asia Minor to the northwest, and Mesopotamia to the northeast. As caravans passed through, they shared information, art ideas, and the latest trade goods. So Palestine became a land-bridge for trade and ideas. Traders used the roads in peacetime and armies in wartime. No matter who was at war in the Near East, much of the fighting was done on Palestinian soil. So for its day, Palestine had a highly advanced set of roads.

The *Via Maris* (mentioned in Isa. 35:8) was the way across Palestine from the Mediterranean. It cut through the Carmel Range at Megiddo. From there it went along the Mediterranean, across sand dunes and swamps southward, and through Sinai to Egypt. The Egyptian kings used this road as their armies marched northward in conquest. For example, Pharaoh Necho was marching along the *Via Maris* on his way to Carchemish on the Euphrates when he was halted at Megiddo by King Josiah of Judah. In their battle, Josiah was killed and Judah suffered a serious defeat.

At Megiddo the *Via Maris* split into two main branches: (1) the

Modern Damascus. Damascus, the capital city of Syria, lies northwest of the Ghuta Plain, a district famous for its orchards and gardens. Damascus is a natural communication center, linking the caravan route with the Mediterranean coast about 105 km. (65 mi.) to the west.

King's Highway. The modern highway winding down into the Arnon Valley closely follows the route of the ancient King's Highway. The original road ran directly from the Gulf of Aqaba to Syria. Edomites and Ammonites closed the road to the Israelites when they tried to enter the Promised Land (Num. 20:17-18).

road to Tyre, Sidon, and Ugarit by the Mediterranean Sea and (2) the road by the Sea of Galilee to Hazor. At Hazor, the road again divided into: (1) a road to the north leading to Aleppo through the Beqa and (2) a road northeast to Damascus.

The *King's Highway* was the second major north-south road of Palestine. This was a mountainous road between Saudi Arabia and Damascus. It ran close to the desert in Transjordan and was rougher than the *Via Maris*. The King's Highway crossed lands that were controlled by Edomites, Moabites, Ammonites, and Israelites. In places it was not at all a "king's highway," for it followed *wadis* (Zered, Arnon, and Jabbok) that were too steep and rough for armies or caravans to travel.

Another road ran part of the way alongside the King's Highway. This road connected Edom to Rabbath-bene-ammon across flat desert land. Although this road helped travelers escape the steep wadis, the lack of water along the way often caused problems.

Other caravan routes joined the King's Highway. From the east came the Dumah and Tema route; from the west a route from Egypt joined at Bozrah. The northern Transjordan enjoyed many contacts with Palestine; several roads ran down the mountains into the Jordan Valley. At shallow places—*fords*—travelers could cross the Jordan and then continue on the road to the cities of Bethshean, Shechem, and Jericho.

Three roads crossed Canaan and Transjordan on the way to Egypt. All of these crossed the desert. The roads were developed in order to span the Arabah, Negev, and Sinai Deserts. From Edom in Transjordan, the way to Shur (Gen 16:7) went down by way of

Bozrah and Pinon from the high country into the Arabah. From there it went through the Wadi Zin (cf. Num. 27:14) and past Kadesh-barnea into the Sinai Peninsula. There a narrow strip of land between the sands and the hills gave access to Egypt. The southern route left Elath by the Gulf of Elath over the R-Tih Plateau to Egypt. The northern route connected Canaan with Egypt by the *Via Maris*; this was a popular route, and most caravans and

---

How a Roman Road Was Built

The Romans were prodigious road builders. They spent five centuries completing a road system that extended to every corner of their empire and eventually covered a distance equal to 10 times the circumference of the earth at the equator. This included over 80,000 km. (50,000 mi.) of first-class highways and about 320,000 km. (200,000 mi.) of lesser roads.

Before the Romans built a road, they conducted a survey. They could calculate distances to inaccessible points, run levels with accuracy, measure angles, and lay out tunnels and dig them from both ends with a vertical shaft. Road surveyors considered the slope of the land and questions of defense. Where necessary (as in the regions of Cumae and Naples), they cut tunnels through mountains with a skill that aroused admiration for centuries. Because Romans tried to build straight roads—often over hills rather than around them—slopes frequently were steep; 10 percent grades were common.

When building an important road, Roman engineers dug a trench the full width of the road and 1.2 to 1.5 m. (4 to 5 ft.) deep. The roadbed was built up with successive layers of large and small stone and rammed gravel; sometimes there was a layer of concrete. Normally roads were surfaced with gravel, which might rest on a bed of mortar. Near cities, in places where traffic was heavy, or in the construction of an important road, engineers paved the surface with large, carefully fitted stones about 30 cm. (12 in.) thick and 45 cm. (18 in.) across.

Stone bridges were usually built where roads crossed streams. Such construction was possible because the Romans had concrete much like that in use today. To make lime mortar set under water and resist water action, the road engineers had to add silica to the mixture. The Romans had large quantities of volcanic sand *(pozzolana)*, which had a mixture of silica in proper proportions.

Unfortunately, records do not tell us how long it took to build Roman roads or how large the road gangs were that built them. The Appian Way—"Queen of Roads" and forerunner of many other Roman roads on three continents—was begun in 312 B.C. as a road for use in the Samnite Wars. The 211 km. (132 mi.) to Capua must have been completed within about a decade. Ultimately, the Appian Way reached southward 576 km. (360 mi.) from Rome to Brundisium on the Adriatic Sea. The road system was gradually extended through the efforts of numerous Roman emperors. Augustus, Tiberius, Claudius, and Vespasian were among those who launched great road-building projects.

Some Roman roads have been used throughout the Middle Ages and into modern times. The Appian Way, on which Paul traveled to Rome (cf. Acts 28:13-15), is still an important artery of western Italy. It is a mute reminder of the glory of the time when all roads led to Rome.

marching armies used it. This is most likely the route Joseph chose when he fled from Palestine with Mary and the baby Jesus when King Herod gave orders for all baby boys to be killed (Matt. 2:14).

MESOPOTAMIA'S WATER AND ROAD SYSTEM

Mesopotamia was the land that lay between the Tigris and the Euphrates Rivers. In the Bible it is called Padan-aram (Gen 25:20; 28:2, 5) or "Aram of the two rivers." This second title is translated in the Greek as *Mesopotamia* (Gen. 24:10). Actually, it included the area from the mountains in the north to the Persian Gulf in the south. Important ways of living developed in this particular region

Roman road. This road between Antioch and Aleppo is 6 m. (20 ft.) wide and made of limestone blocks. Such roads crossed the entire Roman Empire, allowing rapid troop movement and facilitating trade.

between the rivers, just as the Nile River Valley in Egypt gave rise to another important people.

Mesopotamia comprised much of the "Fertile Crescent," which stretched from the Persian Gulf to the Amanus Mountains, an arch of over 1,600 km. (1,000 mi.). The western area of the Fertile Crescent covered only about 800 km. (500 mi.).

The Tigris and Euphrates Rivers were fed by the melting snows of the mountains of Armenia (Ararat). These high mountains drained the melted snow into swamps at the head of the Persian Gulf. The larger of the two rivers, the Tigris, flowed over 1,800 km. (1,100 mi.) with a rapid current that caused a great deal of soil erosion. The Tigris was a very muddy river because of this eroding action. The Euphrates was a slow-moving river over most of its 2,800 km. (1,700 mi.) course. The river was very steep; but because it was also very wide, the flow of water was more gradual.

The two rivers came together in the marshy delta. "The land between the two rivers" was rich when the extra water was drained off; but flooding was common in this area. In the upper valley the opposite was true; the land had to be irrigated.

Farming was Mesopotamia's big business. People of the area had to trade for ore, timber, and metals. Their only local mineral resource was bitumen, used to waterproof boats and form a kind of cement for buildings. Bitumen in this area came from the middle of the Euphrates, where it seeped out like thick oil (Gen. 6:14).

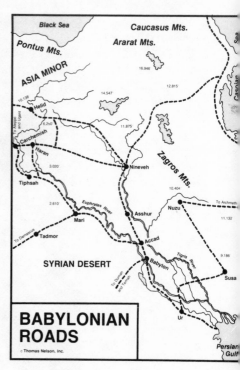

BABYLONIAN ROADS

c Thomas Nelson, Inc.

Mesopotamia was surrounded by mountains on the north and east and by desert on the west and south. Between the two rivers was a steppe—a flat, dry, almost desert-like area. It was about 400 km. (250 mi.) wide. The hills to the north provided streams that flowed downward to the Euphrates. These ran in grooves of rock that had been cut for thousands of years. On the banks of these rivers were the cities of Carchemish, Mari, Maran, and Asshur. When the water supply was good, the steppe provided grain, cattle, sheep, and orchards of fruit.

The middle and lower parts of the rivers could be traveled easily. Small ships used canals. Ships on the Persian Gulf shuttled gold and timber between Babylonia and India.

Inland roads connected Mesopotamia with its neighbors to the north and west. Another road to the south followed the route of the Euphrates. Where the roads crossed, great trading cities grew up. At Mari the road split in 3 directions: (1) To the north it went to Haran, (2) to the northwest it went to Aleppo and Ugarit, and (3) to the southwest it crossed the desert to Tadmor and Damascus.

Another road ran parallel to the Tigris River to Nineveh. At Nineveh, other roads joined it from the northeast (the Caspian Sea) and from the west: One road ran to the northwest through the hill country to Asia Minor. Another ran southwest across the steppe between the rivers and connected Nineveh with Haran and Carchemish. At Carchemish on the Euphrates, this road split into two routes—one going north to Asia Minor and the other going south to Aleppo. Only a few passes connected the Zagros Mountains in western Persia with Mesopotamia. The southern route to the east lay between Ur and Susa. It was often used as an army road, since the Elamites and Babylonians were often at war.

SHIPPING

Forests and natural harbors encouraged shipbuilding in several countries of the ancient world. Phoenicia had both, whereas Egypt and Israel lacked the wood. The cedars of the Lebanon Mountains gave Phoenicia an abundant supply of sturdy wood.

Egypt had the great Nile River, which could be traveled by boat from the Mediterranean Sea to the first cataract at Aswan. Syria and Phoenicia had many bays that were developed into harbors (e.g., Ugarit, Byblos, Sidon, and Tyre). In contrast, Canaan's seashore was unfit for harbors. In spite of this, Canaanites (and later the Israelites) learned to build a seaport wherever a river flowed into the sea, such as at the Yarkon (Tel Kasileh) and the Kishon. They also used small bays at Accho and Joppa. But shipping competition from the north and the Philistines to the southwest hurt Israel's sea development.

The biblical writers were quite familiar with sea travel. Ezekiel calls sailors wise men (Ezek. 27:8). The Psalmist praises God for the ships of the sea (Psa. 104:26). But the Psalmist also knew of the dangers of the sea (Psa. 107:24).

Of course, the Book of Jonah includes much about sailing. The prophet came to the harbor of Joppa and booked passage to Tarshish. A storm broke (Jon. 1:4) and the sailors called on their god (1:5). God rescued them after they threw Jonah overboard and called on God for mercy (1:14).

Ezekiel describes a merchant ship like this: "They have made all thy ship boards of fir trees of Senir: they have taken cedars from Lebanon to make masts for thee. Of the oaks of Bashan they have made thine oars; the company of the Ashurites have made thy benches of ivory, brought out of the isles of Chittim. Fine linen with broidered work from Egypt was that which thou spreadest forth to be thy sail; blue and purple from the isles of Elishah was that which covered thee. The inhabitants of Zidon and Arvad were thy mariners: thy wise men. O Tyrus, that were in thee, were thy pilots. The ancients of Gebal and the wise men thereof were in thee thy calkers: all the ships of the sea with their mariners were in thee to occupy thy merchandise" (Ezek. 27:5-9).

Here Ezekiel uses the usual Hebrew word for ship (*'oniyah*). This word is also used in 1 Kings 9:26-27 and Isaiah 33:21. The phrase "navy of Tharshish" (1 Kings 10:22) signifies a fleet of ships with trading goods from the city of Tarshish—a port often visited by Phoenicians (Ezek. 27:12) and the place to which Jonah tried to escape. The Old Testament also uses the words *sefinah* (Jon. 1:5) and *si* (Isa. 33:21; Num. 24:24) to refer to ships. Barges or floats carried wood and other types of cargo (1 Kings 5:9).

According to Ezekiel, the bottoms of boats were made of fir wood and the masts were sometimes of cedar (27:5). Isaiah adds that the mast was placed in a socket and the ropes were tied to the top of the mast to hold it in place (Isa. 33:23).

Observation posts at the top of the masts were common (Prov. 23:34). Sails were strung from the mast and a covering under the mast protected the sailors from the sun (Ezek. 27:7). They used both sails and oars to power the ships (27:8).

Egypt used ships as its main means of transportation. Inside the country, the Nile and its tributaries made it unnecessary to build many roads. Even between villages small boats were used for travel.

The Egyptians made certain boats with bundles of papyrus reeds, tied with hemp or papyrus. Light and fast, these papyrus

---

The Nile-Red Sea Canal

The idea of a canal linking the Mediterranean and Red seas is about 4,000 years old. The first canal was probably built by Pharaoh Sesostris I (reign 1980–1935 B.C.). Egypt's foreign commerce at that time was a royal monopoly. Middle Kingdom pharaohs believed in courting the favor of their neighbors. Sesostris I or another pharaoh of that era built a canal to increase commerce with his southern neighbors in Punt (possibly modern Somaliland).

During the time of the pharaohs, the Nile River divided into three great branches that passed through the delta and emptied into the Mediterranean Sea. The easternmost branch (which has silted up since the time of Christ) was the branch from which the Nile-Red Sea canal was built. The canal seems to have run from the Nile at Bubastis (modern Zagazig) through the land of Goshen to join Lake Timsah. There it turned south, passing through the Bitter Lake and another canal connecting it with the Red Sea. The earliest written record of the canal is the inscription of one of Hatshepsut's trading expeditions to the Punt. Remains of the canal's masonry work show that it was about 45 m. (150 ft.) wide and 5 m. (16 ft.) deep. The canal gradually fell into disuse.

About 600 B.C., Pharaoh Necho tried to reopen the Nile–Red Sea canal. Herodotus recorded the undertaking: "The length of this canal is equal to a four days' voyage, and is wide enough to admit two *triremes* (war galleys) abreast....In the prosecution of this work under Necho, no less than 10,000 Eyptians perished. He at length desisted from his undertaking, being admonished by an oracle that all his labor would turn to the advantage of a barbarian."

Strabo (*ca.* 63 B.C.–A.D. 21) stated that Darius of Persia carried on the work, then stopped on the false opinion that the Red Sea was higher than the Nile and would flood Egypt. The Ptolemies made the canal navigable by means of locks.

During the Roman occupation of Egypt, Roman Emperor Trajan (reign A.D. 98–117) added a branch to the canal. This later fell into disuse, as the earlier canal had. A Muslim caliph ordered his men to fill in part of the canal as an act of war in A.D. 767, and it was never reopened.

The Suez Canal, opened in 1869, directly linked the Red Sea with the Mediterranean, without using the Nile.

boats were used for personal transportation and not for trade.

The Egyptians had to import wood for shipbuilding; Nubia and Phoenicia sold most of this timber to Egypt. The Egyptians learned to build boats in pieces; they could be taken apart so that they could be carried over land and reassembled. This was especially helpful in wartime. In peacetime, the Egyptians used these boats to open trade with the Red Sea. Ships could be built farther west and carried in pieces to the coast for assembly. History tells us that Queen Hatshepsut of Egypt sent five ocean-going ships to Punt on the African coast in this way. Temple drawings show this fleet brought back to Thebes a load of ivory, ebony, gold, eye paint, skins, and greyhound dogs.

Because water travel kept increasing in Egypt, the armies of Pharaoh Necho dug a canal from one of the branches of the Nile to the Red Sea. In 279 B.C., Ptolemy Philadelphus reopened this same canal. The canal provided water travel for Egypt from Aswan to the Mediterranean, and from the Nile to the Red Sea.

Beni Hasan. A group of Semitic nomads appears before an Egyptian official in this section of a wall painting from a tomb at Beni Hassan (*ca.* 1890 B.C.). The caravan carries merchandise for trade in Egypt. Notice that the men are armed against robbers, who made travel dangerous in the early days.

Egypt learned how to use warships to protect its shores. A "relief drawing" at Medinet-Habu shows the Egyptian ships winning a sea battle against the Philistines and the "Peoples of the Sea." These invaders came from the Aegean Sea and attacked Egypt. The Peoples of the Sea were caught between the fire from Egyptian ships and archers shooting arrows from land. This may well be the earliest record of a naval battle.

Thus ships had two main uses: trade and defense. Pleasure travel was little known. If an extra space on a boat was available, a passenger might go along. Such people paid their fare (Jon. 1:3) and were given a place to sleep.

In Paul's day, people commonly traveled by ships. Paul used ships for his missionary journeys. On his way to Rome, his ship ran on a reef and broke into pieces (Acts 27:41). Since the island of Malta was nearby, everyone reached shore safely (27:44). From there the Romans took Paul on a ship to Rome (Acts 28:11), with stops at Syracuse (28:12) and Puteoli (28:13).

CARAVANS

We are not sure when caravan travel began; surely it must have been early. To make a profit, these strings of pack animals could move large amounts of goods over long distances. At first such long-distance caravans kept to main roads and missed cities along the way. But when man learned to tame the camel, he was able to travel across deserts to otherwise out-of-the-way places. Even today, caravans go to many places that planes and cars do not normally reach.

Each caravan had a leader who controlled the route of the journey. He would make business deals with others who wished to join the caravan for safety. Sometimes a family or tribe traveled the roads as a full-time work, buying and selling along the way. We see an example of this in the story of Joseph, who was sold as a slave to a caravan that passed by. He was purchased by Ishmaelite traders who came "from Gilead with their camels bearing spicery and balm and myrrh, going to carry it down to Egypt" (Gen. 37:25). The caravan people often traveled between Gilead and Egypt.

A picture in the tomb of an Egyptian at Beni Hasan shows such a caravan entering Egypt (*ca.* 1890 B.C.). The 37 members of the caravan were all Semitic and included men, women, and children. They carried eye paint to Egypt, and the caravan was protected by armed warriors with bows, spears, and throw-sticks. Desert regions and mountains were well-known hide-outs for robbers, so bodyguards were a vital part of the caravan company.

The late William F. Albright, an archaeologist, argued that Abraham was himself a caravan leader. The Bible says he had 318 trained bodyguards (Gen. 14:14), and he migrated from Ur to Canaan. He moved around in Canaan, from Hebron to Beersheba, then to Gerar; he even traveled to Egypt during a famine. He most likely traded the products his herds produced for whatever needs he had along the road. But we have no real proof that he was a caravaneer.

Caravanserais grew up. These were roughly equivalent to modern "truck stops," with all the needs of the traveling caravans in mind: food, water, bathing places, and supplies.

These *caravanserais* were usually found at points where roads crossed; some were near harbor cities and others at points where special help was needed, such as a water hole in the desert.

Inns were much like *caravanserais* but smaller, with less help for the traveler. An inn provided hospitality for the night. In the parable of the Good Samaritan, Jesus tells us about the travel from Jerusalem to Jericho (Luke 10:30-37): When a passing Samaritan stopped to help a traveler who had been attacked, he took him to an inn to recover.

A. Camels. By taming the camel, caravaneers shortened their travel routes, for the camel seemed able to go anywhere. Desert conditions that hurt man (dust, lack of water, too much sand, the heat, the rocks, and thorny grass) were natural conditions for the camel.

According to archaeological finds, the two-humped camel was being used as a pack animal in Turkestan in about 3500 B.C. Camels must have been domesticated much earlier than that. The camel also provided milk. Since its strong body could pull a plow or be ridden, it was called "the ship of the desert." Each camel could carry up to 230 kg. (500 lb.) for up to 160 km. (100 mi.) a day.

The patriarchs used camels in their travels. When Abraham

sent his servant to get a bride for Isaac, the emissary went to Padan-aram with a caravan of 10 camels (Gen. 24:10). Jacob left Padan-aram with many camels; his wives and children sat on them (Gen 31:17). Jacob sent a present of 30 milking camels and their colts to Esau (Gen. 32:15-16). The Ishmaelites who took Joseph to Egypt loaded their goods on camels (Gen. 37:25).

The roaming nomads who spent so much of their time in the desert commonly used the camel. The Amalekites, Hagarites, and Midianites especially were camel-raisers. The Israelite tribes took as many as 50,000 camels when they conquered the Hagarites (1 Chron. 5:21). Job owned 3,000 camels—a large herd for any one man to have. His troubles took them from him, but afterward he had twice as many.

The Jews who returned from the Exile brought with them 435 camels (Neh. 7:69). In the New Testament, the wise men most likely rode on camels to see Jesus (Matt. 2:1-12).

B. Donkeys. People who lived in the area we now call Saudi Arabia are credited with taming the donkey sometime around 4000 B.C. Early pictures show the donkey as a farm animal and a caravan worker (painting at Beni Hasan, *ca.* 1890 B.C.). The donkey traveled well across the desert, for he was used to eating thin, thorny grasses that were hard to find. Donkeys often ate coarse food that camels refused to eat.

The Bible mentions the donkey many times. Both rich and poor people owned and rode donkeys.

Camel. Caravans of pack animals moved large quantities of trade goods from place to place in the ancient East. The domestication of the camel allowed traders to go into previously inaccessible areas.

Ziba met David with donkeys and supplies when David was forced to leave Jerusalem (2 Sam. 16:1-2). Solomon equipped his mounted army with horses, so that the donkey came to be used for carrying heavy loads only. Donkeys were used less often as royal beasts of burden, and they were looked down upon. So in prophesying the coming Messiah, Zechariah said He would be riding on a donkey (Zech. 9:9)—a sign that He would be humble.

3

TOOLS AND IMPLEMENTS

The Old Testament often refers to tools by using the collective Hebrew words *keli* (which literally means "vessels" or "instruments") and *hereb* (which refers to a sword, knife, or any sharp cutting instrument). When a scripture uses one of these general terms the context can help us determine which tools the writer might have been referring to. Each craft or trade had its own particular tools.

Tools appeared on the scene of history very early. The Bible tells us that "Cain was a tiller of the soil" (Gen. 4:2). He must have used some kind of tool to break the ground, though the exact tool is not mentioned. Archaeologists have found flint knives, scrapers, and hoes from the early Neolithic era (*ca.* 7000 B.C.) in Palestine. Flint was used for rough tools such as reaping hooks even after metal was plentiful (*ca.* 1000 B.C.). But as metal workers learned to use copper, bronze, and meteoric iron, they developed various metal tools.

Archaeologists have found that woodworkers used metal saws with teeth that pointed toward the handle. These same saws were used for cutting stone (1 King 7:9; Isa. 10:15). Some people were executed by being sawn in two (Heb. 11:37). Tradition has it that Isaiah might have been killed in this manner.

Perhaps the Israelites were not as skilled in the use of tools as some of their neighbors. This might explain why Solomon employed the craftsmen of Hiram to build the temple (1 Kings 7:13), and why Bezaleel and Oholiab were summoned for the building of the tabernacle (Exod. 31:1-11).

GENERAL TOOLS

Scripture refers to two tools that were used in a variety of trades—the axe and the hammer.

Egyptian razor blade. Some of the tools used by ancient barbers were similar to modern-day shaving and grooming devices. This Egyptian razor blade, dating from about the sixteenth century B.C., is made of bronze.

A. Hammer. The ancient hammer looked much like the hammers we use today. More than one Hebrew word was used to denote the hammer. The type of hammer used to drive the tent peg into Sisera's head (Judg. 5:26) was called the *halmuth*. But the Hebrew words *makkubhah* and *makkebheth* also referred to the hammer (Judg. 4:21; 1 Kings 6:7; Isa. 44:12; Jer. 10:4).

B. Axe. Seven different Hebrew words are translated as *axe* in the English versions. The most commonly used is *garzen*, from a Hebrew root word that means "to be cut" or "sever." This type of axe had a head of iron (Isa. 10:34) fastened to a handle of wood by leather straps. The axe head sometimes slipped off the handle during use (Deut. 19:5; 2 Kings 6:4-7).

Axe blades might be short or long. They were set in the wooden handle, parallel or at a right angle to the handle. Materials for the axe head varied from stone (in the earliest times) to bronze and iron. Modern scholars believe that the Israelites learned ironworking from the Philistines (cf. 1 Sam. 13:20).

BARBER'S TOOLS

The types of tools used by barbers in Bible times were much the same as those used today. Barber items such as the razor and mirror are certainly familiar to us (2 Sam. 14:26).

A. Razor. The practice of shaving a man's head after he completed a vow indicates that the Israelites had barbers (Num. 6:9; 8:7; Lev. 14:8; Isa. 7:20; Ezek. 5:1). In some instances the whole body was shaved (Num. 8:7).

Scripture gives us no exact account of what the ancient Hebrew razor looked like, but similar cultures used sharp pieces of obsidian glass and thin flakes of flint. The subject is, however, mentioned by ancient secular writers and illustrated by works of art.

B. Mirror. Mirrors dating from the Bronze Age have been found in Palestine. These mirrors or "looking-glasses" were made of highly polished metal. Hebrew women may have brought mirrors with them when they came out of Egypt. The mirrors used by the Egyptians were made of mixed metals, chiefly copper. These could be polished to a high luster, but were liable to rust and tarnish. The Hebrew word *gillayon* may refer to mirrors (cf. Isa. 3:23). Isaiah considered them to be extravagant finery.

By New Testament times, the Romans had learned to make mirrors of glass. These mirrors often had a cloudy or distorted image (cf. 1 Cor. 13:12).

Tools of the Pharaohs

The Egyptian pyramid is a marvel, even in our modern age. But the question of how it was so precisely constructed has puzzled explorers for centuries.

As the pharaohs' tombs have been excavated, archaeologists have discovered details of Egyptian technology and the tools used in constructing the pyramids. The people of the Nile had a skill for cutting, dressing, transporting, fitting, cementing, and polishing hard and heavy rock. In the pharaohs' tombs, archaeologists have found tools used in the final stages of stone work, along with beautiful flint blades and arrowheads.

Some pyramids were built with iron tools. Colonel Howard Vyse found such a tool in the Great Pyramid—the first clue that the Egyptians used iron. An iron dagger was found in the tomb of King Tutankhamen. In the tomb of a first-dynasty king, archaeologists found scores of knives and swords with wooden blades, along with hoes, axes, and chisels—all fashioned out of metal. The tomb even contained slabs of copper, apparently put there so that copper-

smiths in the "next world" could make more tools for the pharaoh. It seems extraordinary that so much metal would be found in the tomb of a first-dynasty king, but there is no reason to suppose that this hoard was an exception at that time.

Though archaeologists have found some saws in ancient ruins, these are rare discoveries. Saws of ancient Egypt cut on the pulling stroke, not on the pushing stroke as saws do today. Axes, chisels, and saws were commonly used to start wedge-slots in pyramid construction.

Having learned to work with metal, Egyptians were able to develop carpentry skills. They designed wooden chisels, hammers, mallets, scrapers, and squares; several specimens of these tools have been found in the ancient tombs.

While the Egyptians were skilled in the use of tools, the Hebrews were not. The Bible refers to the use of tools only incidentally, in connection with arts and crafts. The tools of the Egyptians surpassed those of other neighboring cultures as well, and enabled Egypt to develop a sophisticated technology that still amazes men today.

BUILDER'S TOOLS

The Hebrew word *bana* was used to refer to construction workers, both skilled and unskilled. The tools used by the master builder as he supervised the construction (1 Cor. 3:10) included the measuring line and the plumb line.

A. Measuring Line. Builders used this tool to survey a building site. Scripture indicates that there may have been more than one type of measuring line. A rope or cord might have been used for this purpose (2 Sam. 8:2; Zech. 2:1); but a string or thread might also have been used. In any case, the measuring line was knotted or marked at one-cubit intervals (cf. 1 Kings 7:15, 23). The cubit (Hebrew, *amma*) was an ancient measure of length that equaled about 45 cm. (17.5 in.). Originally, a cubit was the distance from the tip of the middle finger to the elbow.

In the New Testament, distance was measured in Roman measures (usually translated by the Elizabethan English term *furlongs*), which were approximately 220 m. (660 ft.) long (Luke 24:13; John 6:19; 11:18; Rev. 14:20; 21:16). Sometimes builders took measurements with reeds of a standard length (cf. Rev. 11:1; 21:15).

The measuring line was used as a symbol of God's judgment (Isa. 28:17; Jer. 31:39).

Casting mold. Two axes or chisels rest in a clay mold for casting metal implements. The mold was discovered at Shechem; it dates from about 1800 B.C.

Saw. This copper saw could be fitted into a wooden handle. It is part of a cache of tools discovered at Kfar Monash in Israel.

B. Plumb Line ("Plummet"). The Hebrew word *misqelet* is translated as "plummet" in the KJV of the Bible (2 Kings 21:13). In modern builder's terms, it would be called a plumb line.

A plumb line was used to measure and check the vertical line of a structure. This tool was a small lead cone, fastened by cord to a cylindrical piece of wood that was the same diameter as the cone. The wood cylinder was placed against the wall at the top. If the wall was straight, the lead cone at the end of the plumb line should barely touch the wall.

The plumb line was a symbol of God's action in testing men's lives: "Judgment also will I lay to the line, and righteousness to the plummet" (Isa. 28:17), or as the NIV puts it: "I will make justice the measuring line and righteousness the plumb line."

CARPENTER'S TOOLS

The trade of the carpenter is often mentioned in the Scriptures (cf. Gen. 6:14; Exod. 37). It seems that the carpenter was usually a talented wood carver (1 Kings 6:18, 29). Isaiah mentions the tools of the carpenter's trade: "The carpenter stretcheth out his rule; he marketh it out with a line; he fitteth it with planes, and he marketh it out with the compass, and maketh it after the figure of a man" (Isa. 44:13).

A. Marking Tool. The "rule" mentioned in Isaiah 44:13 was a measuring line, used much the same as we would use a measuring tape or ruler today. After measuring the correct distance on a piece of wood, the carpenter marked it with a stylus or some kind of marking device.

B. Compass or Divider. Ancient carpenters used the compass to mark a circle or portions of a circle. No description of the compass is given in the Scriptures, but archaeologists have found the remains of these ancient tools at several sites in Egypt and Palestine.

C. Adze. In Bible times the adze was used to shape wood (Isa. 44:13). The blade of this tool was curved and attached to the handle at a right angle.

Archaeologists have found the remains of a type of adze used by the Egyptians in about 2000 B.C. This Egyptian adze had a copper blade and was strapped to the wooden handle at a right angle. It is possible that the "planes" mentioned in Isaiah 44:13 were made in the same way.

D. Awl (Aul). Carpenters of Bible times used the awl to poke holes in wood or leather. The awl was a tool with a small pointed blade that stuck straight out the end of the wooden handle. Egyptian monuments picture the awl. The Israelites also used this tool to pierce a hole in the ear of a servant, indicating that he would be a servant forever (cf. Exod. 21:6; Deut. 15:17).

E. Saw. As we have noted, the ancient Egyptians used saws with teeth pointing toward the handle (instead of away from the handle, like those of modern saws). In most cases, these Egyptian saws had bronze blades, attached to the handle by leather thongs. Some ancient saws in the British Museum have blades inserted *into* the handle, much as do our modern knives.

F. Maul or Hammer. The ancient carpenter's hammer was usually made of heavy stone, drilled with a hole for inserting a handle (cf. 1 Kings 6:7; Isa. 41:7). The "maul" mentioned in Proverbs 25:18 is thought to have been a heavy wooden hammer or mallet that the carpenter may also have used (Judg. 5:26).

G. Nail. Carpenters used nails to hold pieces of wood together (Jer. 10:4; Isa. 41:7). Iron was used to make these pins or nails (1 Chron. 22:3). Golden or gilded nails were also used (2 Chron. 3:9).

H. Chisel. Archaeological discoveries show that these sharp tools were made of copper. Looking somewhat like a wide screwdriver, the chisel was a thin wedge of metal and had to be continually resharpened. Copper chisels were used by the Egyptians from about 2000 B.C., and it is very possible that the same tool was used by the Hebrews.

I. Bow Drill. Archaeological discoveries indicate that a type of drill was used in Bible times. The *bit*, or sharp point, was inserted in the tip of a wooden handle. The string of the bow (shaped like the type used to shoot arrows) was wrapped around the wooden handle of the bit. When the carpenter moved the bow forward and backward, it caused the bow drill to rotate, thus boring into the wood.

Scripture makes no specific mention of this tool. However, the Bible does mention boring a hole in the lid of a chest (2 Kings 12:9).

FARMER'S TOOLS

Though Cain was a tiller of the ground (Gen. 4:2), the Bible does not mention specific farming tools until after the Flood. The tools Cain used were probably made of wood and were very primitive.

A. Yoke. Israelite farmers seem to have been well acquainted with plowing, since the yoke is often mentioned in Scripture (e.g., Gen. 27:40).

Farmers placed the yoke on the necks of oxen that pulled the plow. It was made of wood and kept the oxen in their places as they pulled (Deut. 21:3). *Traces* (leather straps) were connected to the yoke and the plow, thus pulling the plow along.

A pair of oxen were called a "yoke" of oxen, as we see in 1 Kings 19:19.

B. Plow. Deuteronomy 22:10 is the first Scripture reference to the plow. The Law admonished, "Thou shalt not plow with an ox and an ass together."

This farming tool was made of wood, though the use of iron was known from the time of Tubal-cain (Gen. 4:22) and the Israelites had iron tools when they entered Canaan (Deut. 27:5).

The primitive Hebrew plow was made of oak. The bent parts were formed by the natural curves in the wood and were held together with iron bands. To this, the farmer fastened a single upright shaft with a short crosspiece to serve as a handle. The single-handed plow was lightweight, allowing the farmer to leave one hand free to use the ox goad.

C. Goad. The Hebrew plowman used a *goad* for urging on the oxen. The goad was a pole 213 to 240 cm. (7 to 8 ft.) long, having a point at one end. The point was sometimes tipped with iron and sharpened (1 Sam. 13:21).

Shamgar used the goad as a very effective weapon: "And after him was Shamgar the son of Anath, which slew of the Philistines six hundred men with an ox goad" (Judg. 3:31).

D. Harrow. The harrow was a well-known farming implement (Job 39:10). Some Scriptures translate this word as "to break the clods," which probably conveys the proper meaning (Isa. 28:24; Hos. 10:11).

The Hebrew noun for "harrow" (*charitz*) represents an instrument with teeth (cf. 2 Sam. 12:31; 1 Chron. 20:3). It might have been pulled along by an ox (Job 39:10). It was actually a kind of sled with stone or metal blades mounted on the underside.

E. Mattock. Israelites used the mattock to break the ground, much as we would use a hoe (Isa. 7:25). The Hebrew word for "mattock" (*ma'der*) literally meant "an instrument used to dig in the ground" (Isa. 5:6).

The head of this tool was made of iron, which could be sharpened (1 Sam. 13:20-21) and used as a weapon.

F. Axe. As we have already noted, the axe was used in various ancient trades. Several Hebrew words are translated as *axe*, and mentioned in connection with the carpenter's work.

The Hebrew word *kardom* probably refers to the "sharpness" of the axe (cf. Judg. 9:48; 1 Sam. 13:20-21; Psa. 74:5). Another Hebrew word, *garzen*, refers to the "cutting power" of the axe (cf. Deut. 19:5; 20:19). A third word, *barzel*, refers to the fact that an axe was made of iron (cf. 2 Kings 6:5).

The axe had a handle of wood. As with the mattock and the goad, it could double as a weapon of war (1 Sam. 13:20).

G. Sickle. Jews used the sickle to harvest grain ("corn") and other crops (cf. Deut. 16:2). This tool had a short wooden handle, turned toward the point. Ancient Egyptian monuments show the type of sickle that was used in Egypt. Clay and wooden sickles with flint blades have been frequently found in excavations.

The reaper grasped the stalks of grain with one hand and cut them off with the sickle, held in the other hand (Isa. 17:5). The sickle is often mentioned in relation to the harvest (cf. Joel 3:13; Mark 4:29).

H. Threshing Machine. After the harvest, the grain was spread on the threshing floor—usually a hard-packed patch of ground located at the outskirts of the city. Farmers separated grain from the straw by having oxen trample on it, or by pulling a threshing instrument over it.

There were two types of threshing machines—one made of flat boards and one that ran on small wheels or rollers (cf. Isa. 28:27-28). The wooden sled-type machine had stones or iron fragments fastened to the underside (Amos 1:3).

Potter's Wheel

The potter's wheel was one of mankind's earliest inventions and has changed surprisingly little in the last 6,000 years. A potter's wheel is not one wheel, but two.

Primitive potter's wheels were made of stone. A disc-shaped stone was placed on the ground; another disc-shaped stone was notched in the center to fit over a pointed pivot in the center of the lower stone. A nudge of the potter's toe set the lower wheel in motion, which rotated the upper wheel. The upper wheel was where the potter shaped his clay.

In Bible times, potter's wheels were also made of wood. The two wheels were joined by a shaft, so that the upper wheel was at hand level. The foot moved the lower disc and the connecting axle caused the upper wheel to revolve. Modern potter's wheels follow the same basic design; some are electrically powered, yet many are turned by foot.

Before using the wheel, a potter must knead his clay to rid it of impurities and air. He "wedges" it—slicing it in half and slamming the halves back together to force out air bubbles. When he feels the clay is ready, the potter places a container of water at his workbench (to keep his fingers wet) and turns to his wheel.

The potter next throws the ball of clay down on the upper wheel. Then he sets the wheel in motion and sur-

rounds the clay with his hands, forcing it true to the center of the wheel head. Now the potter must "master" the clay, making it responsive to his touch. He applies pressure at the base of the clay ball, causing it to rise up in a sort of rounded cone. Then he presses on top of the clay with his thumbs or the palms of his hands. Repeating this three or four times increases the flexibility of the clay and increases its strength.

At this point the potter "opens up" the clay ball by pressing his thumbs into the center, gradually hollowing it out. Applying pressure with his fingers, he evens out the thickness of the cylinder walls. Finally he shapes the clay into a vase, a pitcher, or whatever he chooses.

As the terms *force, master,* and *throw* imply, clay is not always easy to work with. Often a partially formed object will disintegrate into a shapeless heap of clay—perhaps because a tiny stone was overlooked when the clay was worked. The potter must begin to knead the clay again. Or he may dislike the way a pot is forming and sweep it off the wheel in disgust.

Jeremiah 18 describes God as a potter having trouble at His wheel because His people refused to obey Him. This was a familiar image to people in biblical times, because they could see the potter's wheel in the marketplace of virtually every village and town.

I. Fan. After the threshing machine had done its job, the farmers used winnowing fans to throw the stalks and grain into the wind (Isa. 30:24; Jer. 15:7). The breeze separated the grain from the chaff.

The fan is still used in some remote areas of the Middle East. It is a wooden, semi-oval frame, about one meter (one yard) wide, crossed with a texture of hair or palm leaves.

Isaiah 30:24 mentions that a "shovel" was used in the same manner; but this tool is not described.

J. Sieve. Israelites used the sieve to separate grain from the grit and dirt after it was threshed and fanned (cf. Isa. 30:28).

The Old Testament prophets used the sieve as a symbol of God's judgment, which would "sift" the nations (Isa. 30:28; Amos 9:9). Jesus also used this symbolism (Luke 22:31).

K. File. The *file* was used to sharpen other types of tools: "Yet they had a file for the mattocks, and for the coulters, and for the forks, and for the axes, and to sharpen the goads" (1 Sam. 13:21). This is the only scriptural reference to the file, and the exact nature of the tool is not described.

FISHERMAN'S TOOLS

Fish was one of the most abundant foods of Bible times, and we find that fishermen used special tools for catching fish.

A. Casting Net. When Jesus called Simon and Andrew to be His disciples, He found them "casting a net into the sea; for they were fishers" (Mark 1:16-17; Matt. 4:18). The casting net *(amphiblestron)* had a circular form about 4.5 m. (15 ft.) in diameter, with a fine mesh. A fisherman placed lead sinkers around the edge of the net to take the net to the bottom of the lake. He attached a long piece of line to the center of the net. The fisherman held this line by the left hand, gathered the net up in the right hand, and cast it out into the shallow water.

B. Dragnet, or Drawnet *(sagēnē,* Matt. 13:47). Fishermen used this type of net in deeper water (Luke 5:4). It was a long net—sometimes nearly 100 m. (328 ft.) long—and about 2.5 m. (8 ft.) wide. The fisherman attached corks to one side to keep it buoyed up, and lead sinkers to the other side to make it sink.

Sometimes the net was stretched between two boats and the boats were rowed in a circle, drawing the net together. The ropes attached to the bottom of the net were drawn in faster than those at the top, which trapped the fish in the net (John 21:16).

C. Spear. Hebrew fishermen used the spear, and possibly a type of harpoon, for fishing (Job 41:7). The spear head and the barbs of the harpoons were probably made of iron. Ancient inscriptions prove that such tools were used by the Egyptians.

D. Hook. Hooks were also used for fishing. Peter used a fish hook to catch a fish (Matt. 17:27). We know that Assyrian fishermen used the hook and line for fishing, as shown by inscriptions from 700 B.C.

E. Anchor. Ancient fishermen used the anchor much as it is used today. However, early anchors were simply large stones or crooked pieces of wood weighted with stones. These crude tools were not capable of holding a large vessel, and metal anchors with hooks were soon developed.

At first, the metal anchor had only one barb to catch the ground; then anchors with as many as four barbs were developed. Acts 27:29 is thought to refer to a four-barbed anchor: "They cast four anchors out of the stern, and wished for the day."

In ancient times anchors were thrown from either end of the ship (Acts 27:30). When ships were at anchor near the shore, they were placed with their stern to the beach and their bow in deep water, having the anchor cast from the bow.

The anchor has long been a symbol of hope, as we see in Hebrews 6:19. Early Christians used the anchor to signify the successful end of the voyage of life. Thus it is found as an emblem on their tombs.

HOUSEHOLDER'S TOOLS

Hebrew women used special tools in preparing food for the family. Most of the food preparation was done in a courtyard near their houses.

A. Oven. Ovens were usually built in the courtyard. These early ovens were hollow at the top, about 60 cm. (24 in.) in diameter at the base and about 30 cm. (12 in.) high. They often were constructed by alternating layers of clay and potsherds (pieces of broken pottery; Job 2:8). The women could bake flat cakes by sticking them to the sides of the oven or placing them over fire on

Flints and bone tools. Discovered at Jericho, these flints and bone tools date from the Neolithic period (5000–4000 B.C.). Other tools and weapons made of flint were found on the same excavation level. Most appear to have been knife blades, some having fine serrated edges.

heated stones (Lev. 2:4; 11:35; 26:26). Archaeologists have found the remains of such ovens in the ruins of Megiddo.

B. Mill. We first read of the grain mill in Exodus 11:5, which describes the custom of hiring women to turn it: "even unto the first-born of the maidservant that is behind the mill." The wandering Israelites ground *manna* in mills (Num. 11:8). The mill was such an important item of domestic use that no one was allowed to take it as collateral for a loan (Deut. 24:6).

In Abraham's time, grain was pounded or ground by spreading it on a flat stone and rubbing it with a round stone muller (Gen. 18:6). This type of grinding tool was found in the ruins of Jericho.

The rotary mill came into use in the Iron Age. It consisted of two circular stone slabs 50 cm. (20 in.) across. A pivot secured the upper slab (Hebrew, *rekeb*) to the stone beneath. Women poured grain through the pivot hole in the upper stone, and it was ground as the wheel turned. The flour was forced out between the two stones as more grain was added. Often two women would grind, sitting on either side of the mill. They would turn the mill with a wooden handle attached to the outer surface of the upper stone (cf. Matt. 24:41).

C. Needle. Hebrew women used needles to make clothing. The first scriptural reference to needlework is found in Exodus 26:36, which gives specifications for the temple hangings. Needlework was common in Bible times (cf. Exod. 27:16; 28:39; 36:37; 38:18; 39:29; Judg. 5:30; Psa. 45:14).

D. Knife. The Hebrews used a knife called *ma'akeleth* (literally, "eating instrument") for slaughtering animals for food or sacrifice (Gen. 22:6). Another Hebrew word, *hereb*, meant a knife made of flint (Josh. 5:2) or perhaps a knife for shaving (Ezek. 5:1). The flint knife survived well into the Bronze Age for everyday use.

E. Press. Presses were used to extract the juice of grapes, olives, and other fruit. A full winepress was a sign of prosperity.

MASON'S TOOLS

Stone masons used many of the same tools that were used by builders and carpenters of that day, such as the hammer, plumb line, marking tool, measuring line, saw, and chisel.

Masons used saws to cut stone for the temple (1 Kings 7:9). Some Bible passages suggest that they may have used a level and square (cf. Ezek. 41:21), but clear Scripture references to such tools cannot be found. Stones from both Herod's temple and his fortress-palace at Masada show that the stones were cut and fitted before being erected. They often have numbers or mason's marks carved in them.

POTTER'S TOOLS

Until about 3000 B.C., pottery was hand-molded. After this time, it was made on a potter's wheel. The potter's work is described in Jeremiah 18:3-4.

A. Wheel. Examples of the potter's wheel have been discovered in archaeological diggings at Jericho, Megiddo, Gezer, Laish, Hazor, and other Palestinian cities. These relics show that the potter sat at the edge of a pit in which the "wheel" stood (Jer. 18:3). The lower stone of the wheel rested in the pit, while the upper stone was on a pivot. A wooden collar encircled the upper stone, and the potter turned this collar with his feet.

B. Paddle and Scraper. From archaeological finds, we know that the potter used various types of paddles and scrapers of wood and stone. But there is no record of these tools in the Scriptures.

C. Furnace. Furnaces were used for baking pottery. The remains of such furnaces or kilns have been discovered at Megiddo.

METAL SMITH'S TOOLS

In Bible times, the smith was often referred to as "he who blows the coals" (Isa. 54:16). The metal smith poured liquid metal from ladles or buckets into clay molds or beat it on an anvil with a forge hammer. The coppersmith and ironworker *(haras barzel)* were also known as "hammerers" (Isa. 41:7; 44:12), because they flattened and smoothed metal by pounding.

A. Anvil. The Hebrew word for *anvil* is found only in Isaiah 41:7: "And he that smootheth with the hammer inspired him that smote the anvil." The earliest anvils were made of bronze. But

when Israelites mastered the smelting of iron, they formed it into
anvils. The anvil was a metal surface on which the smith would
place an object to hammer it into the desired shape.

B. Bellows. The smith used this instrument to force a draft of
air through clay pipes to the furnace, producing enough heat to
melt metal (Ezek. 22:20). Usually the bellows (Hebrew, *mappuach*)
was made of sewn goat or sheep skin (Jer. 6:22). The skin formed
an airtight bag that was fitted in a frame of wood. When the smith
compressed this bag, the air was forced out under the pressure.

C. Furnace. The smith used a furnace that could be heated to

Bronze implements. These
implements found at
Megiddo were made of
bronze. The Israelites used
the knife for eating and for
slaughtering animals. These
implements were originally
attached to wooden handles.

very high temperatures (cf. Dan. 3:19). But the ancient smiths were never able to get their furnaces hot enough to pour molten iron, as they did copper. Iron came from the furnace as a spongy mass of iron, slag, and cinders. The smith hammered it out to remove the slag and air bubbles. Then it was put in the furnace until it was forged into wrought iron, and finally worked by the skilled blacksmith (1 Sam. 13:18-20). If he needed to sharpen the edges of instruments, such as axes or knives, he might use a whetstone or file (Eccl. 10:10).

Archaeologists have found the remains of smiths' furnaces at Beth-shemesh in Palestine (Josh. 15:10). There were two different types of furnaces, both made of clay bricks. One had holes in the sides where air could be forced in by a blowpipe. The second type was long and narrow, and open to the air.

D. Tongs. Often the smith used tongs to lift iron from the furnace or fire (Isa. 44:12). These early tongs were made of bronze; but as iron became available, they were made of that metal.

The smith's tongs had much the same shape as tongs used today. In the archaeological diggings at Tell el-Amarna, Egypt, tongs from 1350 B.C. have been discovered. The grasping ends on the ancient tongs were shaped like human hands.

Iron plow. Although the Israelites had iron tools when they entered Canaan (Deut. 27:5), they did not use the iron-tipped plow extensively until the tenth century B.C. This iron sheath was found at Tell Beit Mirsim in Palestine. The iron plow greatly increased the yield from the soil.

4

MONEY AND ECONOMICS

The functions of money, finance, and economics may seem very difficult to understand. Actually, they are not. *Money* means anything of value that can be easily transported and exchanged. Coins, currency, and jewels are forms of money. *Finance* is the management of money. *Economics* is the study of what money does.

The Bible contains some interesting sidelights on the development of money. It even gives basic principles for its use and management.

DIVINE OWNERSHIP

God owns everything! He owns the entire universe; everything that was, and is, and may become. "The earth is the LORD'S, and the fullness thereof; the world, and they that dwell therein" (Psa. 24:1). He rules over all: "Say among the heathen that the LORD reigneth: the world also shall be established that it shall not be moved: he shall judge the people righteously" (Psa. 96:10).

When God gave the Israelites the land of Canaan as an inheritance, He said: "The land shall not be sold for ever: for the land is mine; for ye are strangers and sojourners with me" (Lev. 25:23; cf. Exod. 15:17-18). This made them *stewards* or caretakers of the land. Ever after, the people of Israel were expected to use their possessions as a sacred trust. This understanding applied to their property, their money, and everything else that they treasured. All belonged to God.

We see the Israelites speak of divine ownership from time to time throughout their history. But we should remember that it was always in the background of their thinking. Jesus spoke directly to this issue in many of His sermons.

MONEY

In the distant past, there were no paper money or coins. People *bartered*—in other words, they traded one thing of value for another. The precious metals gold, silver, and copper were often traded. Later, these metals were made into standard coins. The

Table of measures. These ancient tables of measure are from Nippur, a city of Babylonia founded about 4000 B.C. The table at top lists measures of surface and length and weights; the table at bottom shows measures of capacity.

Bible does not tell us about the steps of this development. Rather, it shows that both systems of trade—barter and coinage—were in use about the same time.

A. Barter. Abram's wealth was counted in cattle, camels, other livestock, servants, silver, and gold (Gen. 13:2; 24:35). Cattle were a common form of money. They were a unit of trade especially well suited to Abram's way of life, for "not knowing whither he went," he followed the Lord's directions (Heb. 11:8). Pharaoh "entreated Abram well" because he believed that Abram's wife was actually his beautiful "sister." Pharaoh gave him sheep, oxen, donkeys, camels, and male and female servants (Gen. 12:14-16). Later, in an identical situation Abram (now called Abraham) again declared his wife Sarai (now called Sarah) to be his sister. Abimelech of Gerar, after learning the deception, returned Sarah to her husband and gave him sheep, oxen, and male and female slaves as an indemnity. In addition he gave Abraham "a thousand pieces of silver" (Gen. 17:5, 15; 20:14-16).

Jacob worked 14 years to pay the dowry for his two wives; he acquired a fortune in cattle, sheep, goats, camels, and donkeys by further labor (Gen. 29:30). King Mesha of Moab was a sheep breeder who paid tribute to Jehoram, the king of Israel—100,000 lambs and the wool of 100,000 rams annually (2 Kings 3:4). Solomon traded 20,000 kors of crushed wheat, 20,000 kors of barley, 20,000 baths of wine, and 20,000 baths of oil annually for cedar, cypress, and algum timber from Lebanon (2 Chron. 2:10). The governors of Judah before Nehemiah taxed the people in "bread and wine, beside forty shekels of silver" (Neh. 5:15).

B. Pieces of Metal. The word *money* appears in the KJV of the Old Testament 112 times as the translation of the Hebrew word for silver. (The same word refers 287 times to objects made of silver.) Silver was a common unit of trade in ancient Israel. Merchants often exchanged small pieces of the metal to cinch a deal, as in the case of Jacob's dowry.

In the New Testament the Greek word for silver is translated 11 times as *money*, 9 times as *pieces of silver*, and 3 times as a general indication of material wealth.

The value of the silver pieces was determined by weight. When Abraham bought the cave of Machpelah he "weighed to Ephron the silver, which he had named in the audience of the sons of Heth, four hundred shekels of silver, current money with the merchant" (Gen. 23:16). This transaction would have been made at the gate of the city, in the presence of witnesses. Jeremiah also weighed out the price of the land he bought from his relative and signed and sealed the deed (Jer. 32:9-10). David paid 50 shekels of silver to Araunah (Ornan) the Jebusite for his threshing floor, his oxen, and the instruments of threshing to make a sacrifice to the Lord (2 Sam. 24:24; cf. 1 Chron. 21:25). Likewise, the Queen of Sheba gave Solomon a gift of 120 talents of gold (1 King 10:10).

Many kings required their subjects to pay an annual levy of silver or gold. For example, Solomon had an income of 666 talents of gold (1 Kings 10:14-15). Hezekiah was forced to pay Sennacherib 300 talents of silver and 30 talents of gold (2 Kings 18:14).

Jacob paid Hamor 100 *qesitah* of silver for a piece of land at Shechem (Gen. 33:19; Josh. 24:32). The Hebrew root for this word is unknown today; the Septuagint translates it "lamb." Perhaps this was the shape of the weight used in weighing out the silver; or perhaps the unit was a quantity of silver equal to the price of a lamb. Whatever it may have been, the name indicates that the biblical writers were thinking of the relative value of goods though the medium was silver.

C. Coinage. Archaeologists have found many ancient coins and coin inscriptions that show us how early coinage appeared. A gold talent and two gold half-talents were found in a twelfth-century grave at Salamis, Cyprus. Egyptian wall paintings depict Cretans and Syrians offering copper ingots in tribute to Pharaoh Thutmose III (1501–1447 B.C.).

If we carefully examine Scripture, we can see the transition from barter to coinage. Joseph was sold for "twenty pieces of silver" to Ishmaelite traders (Gen. 37:28). This meant that the price was 20 shekels of silver by weight. The *shekel* was a weight unit in the payment of silver; the word was so common that it was often omitted. An example of this omission is when Scripture says that the sons of Jacob took "money" (silver) to buy grain in Egypt (Gen. 4:25, 27).

Standard coins gradually replaced these standard units of weight. The early Egyptians, Semites, and Hittites shaped gold and silver into bars, rings, and rounded nodules for convenience of exchange.

In the area of the Aegean Sea, a unit called a *talent* that had the value of an ox became the standard. These ox-talents were pellets or rings of gold weighing 8.5 grams (.29 oz.). A copper ingot of the same value weighed 25.5 kg. (60 lbs.).

The story of Joseph indicates that the patriarchs used silver pieces of a shekel weight. For this reason, Achan had no difficulty knowing the value of the gold and silver he stole from the spoil of Jericho (Jos. 7:21).

God decreed that "the shekel of the sanctuary" must be 20 gerahs (Num. 3:47). Since God was the true King, His priests and prophets were guardians of the money standards. "Ye shall do no unrighteousness in judgment, in meteyard, in weight or in measure," wrote Moses. "Just balances, just weights, a just ephah, and a just hin, shall ye have" (Lev. 19:35, 36*a*).

Honesty in weights and measures was even a part of Israel's law of holiness. The use of different weights (some true and some false) was absolutely forbidden in both the Law and the Prophets (cf. Deut. 25:13-16; Prov. 11:1; 20:10; Hos. 12:7; Amos 8:5; Mic. 6:10-11).

The table of weights and measures on page 67 shows approximate equivalents of the weights and measures used in Old Testament times. Ezekiel tells us the *bath* (liquid) and the *ephah* (dry) are equal in size (45:11-14).

Thirty Pieces of Silver

One of the most infamous stories of the Bible is that of Judas Iscariot, the disciple who betrayed Christ for 30 pieces of silver. While it is difficult to determine exactly what 30 pieces of silver was worth, we know it was not a fortune.

The Roman *denarius* was the most common coin used during Jesus' day. Struck from silver, this coin bore an imprint with the head of the emperor. Because of this, the Jewish people were not allowed to use coins as offerings in religious services; they converted their coins to pieces of silver. Money changers converted the *denarius* or *shekel* for a fee of 12 percent.

The denarius would be worth about 20 cents in today's market, according to its silver weight and content. But one denarius equaled a day's wages of a common laborer at that time, so it had significant buying power. Even so, by this estimate we find that Judas betrayed Christ for a month's salary—hardly a fortune.

The Book of Zechariah prophesied that such an amount would be paid for the Messiah (Zech. 11:12). When Judas accepted 30 pieces of silver for the life of Christ, he fulfilled the prophecy (Matt. 26:15). The amount was also the typical price of a slave or servant during that time.

For the return of his unfaithful wife, Hosea had to pay a homer and a lethech of barley (Hos. 3:2). Solomon bought lumber from Hiram for thousands of cors (kors) of grain and thousands of baths of oil and wine.

Religious fees also had to be paid; this amount was determined by the ritual service performed. For example, a man who had been cleansed of leprosy was required to pay two male lambs, a ewe, an ephah of fine flour, and a log of oil (Lev. 14:19). If a man dedicated himself to the Lord in a vow, the priest charged him according to his age. Males between 20 and 60 paid 50 shekels; those over 60 paid 15; those between 5 and 20 paid 20; and those between one month and 5 years paid the reduced rate of 5 shekels. Women between 20 and 60 were charged 30 shekels. Those above 60 were charged 10 shekels. Those from 5 to 20 had to raise 10 shekels; and those from one month to 5 were let off for 3 shekels (Lev. 27:2-9).

The very poor were charged according to what the priest thought they could pay. Such persons would be charged according to the value of their labor. Indeed, he might serve out his payment by working in the tabernacle under the priests (Lev. 27:2-9).

These passages illustrate why we cannot know when Israel changed from barter measurements to standard coinage. The earliest coins were named for the standard barter measures they represented. Often the Bible uses these terms without saying whether or not they refer to coins.

1. In the Old Testament. The first statement in the Old Testament that explicitly refers to coins is in regard to the 20 gold bowls worth 1,000 "drams" (darics), which Ezra carried to Jerusalem in 458 B.C. (Ezra 8:27). The *daric* was a Persian gold coin that derived

Silver drachma. Bearing the likeness of Alexander, this silver coin was found at the treasury of Persepolis. Coinage first appeared in Asia Minor in the seventh or sixth century B.C.

Coin of Vespasian. A mourning Jew and Jewess flank a palm tree (symbol of Judea) on the reverse of this coin bearing the likeness of Emperor Vespasian. Vespasian and his son Titus conquered Judea in A.D. 70 and the coin was struck in honor of their victory.

its name from Darius I (521–486 B.C.). It weighed 8.4 grams (0.3 oz.), just a little over a shekel.

Archaeologists believe that the kings of Lydia were the first to coin money; they began doing this in the seventh or sixth century B.C. The Persians adopted coinage from the Lydians when they conquered Asia Minor. Thus the value of freewill offerings given for the rebuilding of the temple in 537 B.C. is said to have been 61,000 darics (Ezra 2:69). The recorded value of the gold contributed for the temple in David's time is also given in darics (1 Chron. 29:7); apparently a later historian inserted this information, giving the value of the contribution in terms of the currency used after the Exile.

Archaeologists have found some coins with the marking *YHD* (Judah), indicating that the Persian court authorized their production in that province. These coins are of Greek style, indicating that they were made by Persian governors; the Jews would have considered it idolatrous to mint coins stamped with the images of their rulers. The Bible does not mention these coins.

The Maccabean kings of Judea issued coins after 138 B.C., when the Seleucids granted them full sovereignty. The first Maccabean coins were silver; but since silver coinage was considered an exclusive privilege of the Roman emperor, later coins were made of copper. The first coin issued under this arrangement celebrated "Jerusalem the Holy." It bore the emblem of a chalice on the face and a three-branched pomegranate on the reverse. These Jewish coins generally used symbols from nature or depicted articles used in the tabernacle and temple.

2. In the New Testament. In New Testament times, the silver coin of Tyre and Sidon was called the "temple coin." It was widely known for its pure metal. But the Roman *denarius* quickly superseded all silver coins of the same value. A *denarius* was a soldier's daily wage and worth about 44 cents today. It was the wage mentioned in the parable of the laborers in the vineyard (Matt. 20:9-10, 13). This coin was also used to pay tribute to the emperor. Jesus recognized it as being Caesar's due (Matt. 22:19-21).

The Greek silver coin of the same value was the *drachma*. This was probably the coin in the parable of the lost coin (Luke 15:8).

As we have already noted, the Greek word for *silver* was frequently used for money. Jesus told His disciples to take no "money" (silver) with them when He sent them out two by two (Luke 9:3). Judas was paid 30 "pieces of silver" to betray Jesus (Matt. 26:15; 27:3, 5). These references cite Zechariah 11:12-13, which did not refer specifically to coins.

One of the most famous givers in the New Testament was the poor widow (Mark 12:41-44). She dropped two *lepta*, which equaled the value of a *kodrantēs*, into the temple treasury. The *lepton* was first minted by the Maccabees while the *kodrantēs* was the tiniest Roman copper coin. The *kodrantēs* was about one-sixteenth of a soldier's daily pay. Yet the widow's gift prompted Jesus' highest praise: "Verily I say unto you, That this poor widow hath cast more in, than all they which have cast into the treasury: For all they did cast in of their abundance; but she of her want did cast in all that she had, even all her living" (Mark 12:43b-44).

When the temple tax collector in Capernaum asked the disciples of Jesus if He paid the two-drachma tax, Jesus sent Peter to catch a fish, in whose mouth he found a coin. This coin was a *stater*—a four-drachma piece. It was sufficient to pay the tax for both of them.

Asked whether it was lawful to pay tribute to Caesar, Jesus said: "Show me the tribute money" (Matt. 22:19). The tax coin or *denarius* was shown to Him. It had the image of the emperor on its face.

3. In the Roman Era. Many other coins that are not mentioned in the New Testament still survive from the Roman era. Some of these bear witness to the history of the Jewish people. An example of this is a coin bearing the inscription of "Herod the King," or Herod the Great. This king's soldiers killed all the male babies in Bethlehem under two years of age, to make sure they eliminated the One who was "born King of the Jews" (Matt. 2:2-16).

Some coins bear the inscription *Herod Ethnarch*, referring to Archelaus, who succeeded his father without the title of king. When

Archelaus was deposed and banished, Judea became a Roman province ruled by procurators appointed by Rome.

Herod Antipas built Tiberias, which became the capital of the Roman province of Galilee shortly before Jesus began His ministry. A coin bears his portrait and title on the face, and the inscription *Tiberias* on the reverse. Herod Antipas also beheaded John the Baptist (Luke 9:7, 9) and participated in the trial of Jesus (23:8-12).

Herod Agrippa I minted a coin bearing his portrait with the inscription, "King Agrippa the Great, friend of Caesar." Agrippa persecuted the church; he beheaded James and imprisoned Peter. Luke recorded his agonizing death under the judgment of God. (Agrippa's officials minted another coin in Caesarea to mark the great prize fights, during which he suddenly fell ill.)

Some scholars have disputed Paul's reference to a Roman official called the *anthupatos* on the island of Cyprus (Acts 13:7). But a coin from Cyprus bears the head and superscription of Claudius Caesar on the face, and on the reverse the inscription, *Commenius Proculus anthupatos*. Paul visited Cyprus during the reign of Claudius.

Many other coins support the disputed accuracy of Luke. They confirm the existence of the *Asiarchs* or "chief (people) of Asia," who were listed among Paul's friends in Ephesus (Acts 19:31). Coins also confirm the fact that Philippi was a Roman colony and the chief city of Macedonia (Acts 16:12), and that Tarsus was "no mean city" (21:39).

FINANCE AND ECONOMICS

The principles that control economics—the production, distribution, and consumption of the material means of satisfying human desires—are the same as those that direct finance, the management of an enterprise. The Bible provides useful guidance on all of these issues.

In God's first appearance to man, He let man know that the earth was good and delightful, and it was to be used to meet his needs (Gen. 1:29). But man's enjoyment of life should come from God, not from the things God had made! God Himself was to be the focus of man's desire and attention.

A. The Tithe. When he returned from destroying the Mesopotamian kings, Abraham gave Melchizedek the priest a tenth of the spoil (Gen. 14:20). This was his confession that God was his Lord and the Giver of victory (14:19).

Jacob recognized the same responsibility. He vowed to give God a tithe of all that he received if God would protect him in this journey and return him to his land. This humble confession of dependence on God stands against the proud boast, "My power, and the might of mine hand hath gotten me this wealth" (Deut. 8:17; cf. Dan. 4:30). There was no middle road between these paths.

The giving of a tithe was man's acknowledgment that he is a steward of God's creation. The Old Testament clearly demonstrates that every spiritual relationship of man is expressed in some material way. Rites of worship gave the Israelites a way to confess the operation of their faith in every sphere—not the least of which was the economic sphere.

Israel came out of Egypt by faith in the promises of God. God then claimed the firstborn of Israel (Exod. 13:11-16) and commanded that they be redeemed by the payment of 5 shekels per male child (Num. 3:46-47). This token payment reminded the people of Israel that they belonged to the Lord; they were not their own (cf. 1 Cor. 6:19-20).

God brought the Israelites into the land promised their fathers (Exod. 6:8), where He would rule over them forever (15:17-18). God would drive out the inhabitants and give the land to them (Exod. 23:28-30). In return, they would acknowledge His bounty by offering to Him the firstborn of all clean animals and the first ripe grain and fruits, at the place He would choose (Deut. 12:11-12, 17-18). There they would bring annual tithes of the fruits of the ground and of the flock (Deut. 26:1-12).

When the Israelites offered their tithes, they confessed God's providence to their forefathers, His deliverance in their time of need, His redemption of them from oppression, and His gift of the land of Canaan (Deut. 26:5-9). They invited the Levites, the poor, the widows, and the orphans of their local community to join them at the central sanctuary as they made these offerings to the Lord. No man could appear at a feast empty-handed. The Law required each man to bring an offering proportionate to the way he had been blessed (Deut. 16:10, 17).

Notice the economic dimension of Israel's worship. They offered the Lord a large part of their time; they presented the first fruits of their grain and livestock; they came to the feasts with offerings and tithes; they made freewill offerings of their lives and property; and they gave liberally for the building of the tabernacle and temple. When they returned with booty taken in battle, they set aside a portion for the Lord and Levites before dividing it among themselves (Num. 31:26-54). Their devotion to God cost them the best of all they had (cf. 2 Sam. 24:24). The tithe clearly expressed this costly devotion.

B. Property Rights. Every family received a tract of land as a perpetual inheritance. This land was a trust from the Lord. It enabled every family to produce enough for their own needs and share with their neighbors—especially the poor and strangers living among them. The land remained the Lord's (Lev. 25:23), al-

TABLE OF WEIGHTS AND MEASURES**

UNIT	Equivalents (approx.) Metric	English
*UNITS OF WEIGHT		
bekah, ¹/₂ shekel	1.9 gram	.067 oz
shekel, 20 gerahs	3.8 gram	.134 oz
maneh, 50 shekels	.57 kg	1¹/₄ lbs
talent, 3000 shekels	34.02 kg	75 lbs
UNITS OF VOLUME (LIQUID)		
log	.32 liter	.67 pt
hin	6.5 liter	1.7 gal
bath, ephah, ¹/₁₀ homer	37 liter	10 gal
cor (kor), homer, 10 baths	370 liter	100 gal
*UNITS OF VOLUME (DRY)		
omer, ¹/₁₀ ephah	4 liter	0.45 pk
ephah, ¹/₁₀ homer	40 liter	1.1 bu
lethech, ¹/₂ homer	200 liter	5¹/₂ bu
cor (kor), homer, 10 baths	400 liter	11 bu
cab (kab)	2.2 liter	2 qt

*Tables for gold and silver differed, as did the actual weights of light or normal shekels.

**Based on Collier's Encyclopedia, Vol. 23, ed. by William D. Halsey (New York: Crowell-Collier Publishing Company, 1965), p. 394.

though He gave each family the right to produce food and clothing from it.

The Israelites were to exercise stewardship of the land. They were to use the land and its products unselfishly for those in need around them. Even the passer-by on the road was free to gather grain or fruit to satisfy his hunger (Deut. 23:24-25). They were to be gracious and bountiful to others, just as God had been bountiful to them.

C. Care of the Poor. The welfare of the individual was primarily the responsibility of the family. The closest male relative, known as the kinsman-redeemer, was the protector of the individual. He was to "avenge his blood" and redeem his kinsman from indebtedness (Num. 35:12, 19; Lev. 24–26).

The most notable example of the kinsman-redeemer was Boaz, who bought from Naomi all that had belonged to her husband and married her widowed daughter-in-law, Ruth. Thus Naomi was no longer obligated to Ruth and Boaz for her daily provision. Her property was eventually given to the child of Ruth, the heir of Naomi's son, Mahlon.

Any crops that grew during the sabbatical year and the Year of Jubilee were set aside for the poor to gather. This made the poor responsible to gather their own grain. Thus they preserved their personal dignity and self-respect.

The Law called upon the people in each community to take personal interest in the poor and give them individual encouragement. The third-year tithe was to be stored for the poor of the community, so that they "shall eat and be satisfied; that the LORD thy God may bless thee in all the work of thine hand which thou doest" (Deut. 14:29b; cf. 12:11-12; 26:1-19). Thus the Jewish congregation showed interest in the needy. This practice also helped to prevent division between the comfortable middle-class farmer and the gleaning poor.

The Law told individuals how to deal with neighbors in progressive stages of poverty (Lev. 25:35-43). If a poor man lost all sense of security, his neighbor was to treat him with hospitality, as if he were a stranger or sojourner (Lev. 25:23). If a poor man needed to borrow money, he was not expected to pay interest or return more goods than he borrowed. If the poor man became so indebted that he had to sell himself as a bond servant, he was to be treated as a

MONEY AND ECONOMICS 69

hired servant. He remained a free man (cf. Deut. 15:18), and in the Year of Jubilee he would be freed. Further, the master was obligated to share with him grain, livestock, and wine (Deut. 15:14).

The Law calls the poor man "your brother" (Lev. 25:35, 39). He was a fellow Israelite; but more importantly, he was a brother in God's covenant. For this reason, an Israelite was not to begrudge the bond servant his freedom nor the goods he gave him.

The fourth commandment required a man to let his servants rest on the Sabbath, just as he refreshed himself. He was to pay his hired servants at the end of the day (Lev. 19:13).

The Lord promised that if Israel faithfully obeyed His commandments, there would be no poor in the land because He would bless them (Deut. 15:1-5). But notice the condition of the promise: "There shall be no poor among you; for the LORD shall greatly bless thee.... Only if thou carefully hearken unto the voice of the LORD thy God" (Deut. 15:4-5). If God's people listened, they would be so prosperous that they would lend their wealth to many nations (15:6).

D. Solomon's Reign: An Era of High Finance. Solomon engaged in an extensive building program. This work demanded a complex organization of men, the gathering of imported building materials, and the accumulation of wealth.

At the beginning of his reign, Solomon loved the Lord and walked in His statutes (1 Kings 3:3). In response to his request, God gave him great wisdom (1 Kings 4:29-30). With this wisdom, Solomon organized his people, made international covenants for materials, collected wealth, and pursued his building programs. He gave his most careful attention to the building and dedication of the temple, for that was the central event of his life.

Solomon began by making a mutual trade agreement with Hiram (Huram), king of Tyre, to buy cypress, cedar, and algum lumber. He paid for it with wheat, barley, oil, and wine (1 Kings 5:2-12; 2 Chron. 2:3-10). Solomon drafted 30,000 woodcutters from Israel and sent 10,000 of these men to Lebanon. They worked on a regular schedule: one month in Lebanon and two months at home.

Needing more workers, Solomon made slaves out of the Canaanites who remained in Israel. Of these, 70,000 worked in transportation, 80,000 were stone cutters, and 3,600 were overseers.

As Solomon's kingdom expanded, he demanded tribute from the kings of the territories he conquered (2 Chron. 9:13). Solomon also collected money from merchants who used Israel's trade routes (9:14).

Solomon's merchants bought chariots from Egypt and sold them to the kings of the Hittites and Syria (1 Kings 10:28-29). They built a fleet of ships, manned them with Israelite sailors and the sailors of Hiram, and sent them to Ophir. These men returned with 420 talents of gold. From sources other than the Bible we learn that Solomon conducted a large mining and smelting enterprise in the Sinai Desert. As a result, silver became common in Jerusalem (2 Chron. 9:20, 27; 1 Kings 10:27).

By the end of his life, Solomon had turned his heart away from the Lord. His extravagant living soon brought disaster to the realm. Indeed, 10 tribes broke away from Rehoboam to form the kingdom of Israel under Jeroboam (1 Kings 12:16-24).

The Bible says nothing about the care of the poor under Solomon's reign, nor about the sabbatical year or the Year of Jubilee.

In one generation, the agrarian economy of Israel had become a highly organized state machine. By concentrating the control of labor and the means of production in the hands of a government, Solomon sowed seeds of discontent among his people.

Solomon controlled kingdoms from the Euphrates to the Nile. He saw an end to the devastating wars of David's rule. But he achieved only a meager part of the promised reign of righteousness and peace (Psa. 72).

E. The Divided Kingdom. The economy of united Israel depended upon its agriculture and its control of the trade routes. But during the period of the divided kingdom, Syria became strong, and took from Israel all the pasture lands east of the Jordan and the plain of Galilee and Jezreel. To Jehoahaz, Syria left but a little circle of land around Samaria. Indeed, Israel was reduced to poverty and near collapse (2 Kings 13:3, 22; 14:26).

But by the time Jeroboam II ascended the throne, God had weakened Syria internally. The Syrian kings were worried by the rise of Assyria. This enabled Jeroboam to restore Israel's former borders (2 Kings 14:25-26). By regaining control of the trade routes, he made Israel prosperous once more.

But the new wealth was concentrated in the hands of a few rich people, who lived in luxury and oppressed the poor (Hos. 12:7-8; Amos 2:7-8; 4:1-7, 11; 8:4-60; Mic. 2:1-2). Prophets denounced the rulers and merchants for enriching themselves at the expense of the helpless poor. They predicted that the kingdom would crumble and fall before the powerful Assyrian armies.

By God's grace, the kingdom of Judah continued 150 years longer than the northern kingdom of Israel. But Judah's kings frequently broke their loyalty to the Lord by making treaties with pagan powers. They lost God's promised blessings, weakened their strategic position, and brought military destruction on themselves (cf. 2 Chron. 16:1-10; 1 Kings 16:7-9; 2 Chron. 28:20). Prophets denounced these elders of Judah and princes of the house of David for their injustice and oppression of the poor (Isa. 3:13-14; 10:1-4; Mic. 2:1-2; Jer. 22:1-5).

God had promised Moses that He would bless the land if Israel was obedient. But Israel was not obedient. The rulers no longer held the land in trust for the welfare of the people. Rather, they were using their power to enrich and glorify themselves. They perverted the entire economic system.

The prophets believed the divided kingdom was doomed. But

Stone shekel weights. These Israelite stone weights were used to determine the value of gold and silver. The smaller stone equals the weight of one shekel; the larger equals four shekels. Archaeologists have discovered several stones of this type, most dating from the seventh century A.D.

they believed the Lord would raise up another David who would shepherd the flock in righteousness (Jer. 23:5-6; Ezek. 34:23-25). This new David would proclaim good news to the afflicted and liberty to the captives (Isa. 11:4-5; 61:1-3). He would do what the Davidic kings had failed to do (Psa. 72), and would devote the unjust gains of the world to the Lord (Mic. 4:1-13; Isa. 60:1-12).

F. The New Testament Era. The New Testament affirmed that God is the final authority over every part of our lives. Jesus and the apostles dealt with money, finance, and economics as areas of privilege and responsibility for the people of God.

1. The Economic Teachings of Jesus. Jesus proclaimed good

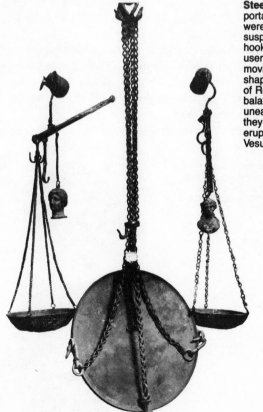

Steelyards. These portable balances were designed to be suspended from a hook or from the user's hand. Note the movable weights shaped like the heads of Roman gods. These balances were unearthed at Pompeii; they were buried by an eruption of Mount Vesuvius in A.D. 79.

news to the poor and liberty to the captives (Luke 4:16-19). He called people to demonstrate their single-hearted devotion to God in their economic pursuits (Matt. 6:19-21, 24). With profound simplicity, Jesus pointed out that God clothes the plants with beauty and gives the birds their food—and so will He care for the needs of His people. He insisted that His followers seek to live in righteousness, for then "all these things shall be added unto you" (Matt. 6:33).

When Jesus sent His disciples out to preach, He commanded them to take no money with them. He insisted that each man would be worthy of his support (Matt. 10:1-10). Thus He taught that the children of the Kingdom should support His servants with their material goods. Jesus demonstrated His own devotion to the will of God by refusing to lay up material wealth for Himself (cf. Luke 9:58). He was the King of kings, yet he lived like a pauper in His own world.

Jesus' life demonstrated that every spiritual condition has a material manifestation. For example, Jesus and His disciples had a common treasury; the responsibility for handling it was given to one of the group, Judas Iscariot. The unfaithfulness of Judas in this task (which they dubbed the "least") revealed his unworthiness to be entrusted with true riches (Luke 16:10-11; John 12:6).

Jesus made it clear that His true children distinguish themselves from hypocrites by the way they minister to their brothers who are in need (Matt. 25:31-46). He did not teach some new doctrine of material goods or try to establish a new economic system. He came to affirm the law of Moses, not to destroy it. The difference lay in who He was: He was the Lord of glory who became a man and lived in perfect obedience to the law of God.

2. The Apostles' Principles. The apostles reaffirmed that God created all things through Jesus Christ for Himself (Col. 1:16). All things have their origin, continuation, and goal in Him (Rom. 11:36). Believers exist for Him (1 Cor. 8:6); they were purchased to glorify Him with their bodies (6:20).

The apostles taught that, since Christ laid down His life for us, we ought to lay down our lives for the brethren (1 John 3:16). This means that if we have this world's goods and see a brother in need, we should love him in deed by sharing our goods with him (1 John 3:17-18).

The early church displayed its stewardship by placing its goods in the care of the apostles (and later the deacons) for distribution as people had need (Acts 2:44-45; 4:32-37; 6:1-7).

Paul asked the churches of Asia Minor and Greece to share their wealth with the needy church of Jerusalem. He wrote, "For I mean not that other men be eased, and ye burdened" (2 Cor. 8:13).

In other words, Paul made it clear that he expected each congregation to give according to its ability. God gives abundance to one so that he may supply the want of another (2 Cor. 8:14). This is why Paul was so grateful for the gift he received from the Philippians. It demonstrated their liberality, it was the fruit of their love, and it was pleasing to God (Phil. 4:10-19).

James approved of Christians' engaging in business for profit; but he reminded them that their first concern should be the will of God. Anyone who failed to follow this course, he said, is boastful and arrogant (James 4:12-16). James also rebuked his fellow Christians for failing to pay their laborers adequately. He said that riches acquired through stinginess would rust, and the rust would witness against them in the day of judgment (James 5:2-4). Paul spoke more positively. He instructed the rich to store for themselves a spiritual treasure by doing good works and sharing their material goods (1 Tim. 6:17-19).

John heard the heavenly choir singing: "Thou art worthy, O Lord, to receive glory and honor and power: for thou hast created all things, and for thy pleasure they are and were created" (Rev. 4:11). At the end of John's Book of Revelation we see the kings of the earth bringing their glory to the new heaven and the new earth (Rev. 21:24, 26). Thus the fruits of man's toil would be remembered and celebrated in the presence of God to all eternity.

5

FORMS OF GOVERNMENT

When God created all things, He brought into being an orderly universe. With the creation of man and the multiplication of people throughout the earth, God ordained government for societies and nations.

When the people of Israel became a nation, government became a necessity. Various forms of government existed throughout their history.

THE THEOCRACY IN THE WILDERNESS

After God rescued His people out of slavery in Egypt, He brought them to Mount Sinai, where He organized them into a nation. He constituted them "a kingdom of priests" (Exod. 19:6) with Himself as their ruler. (The term *theocracy* comes from two Greek words, *theos*, God, and *kratos*, rule, thus rule by God.) From that time on, Israel would always consider itself to be God's kingdom and God to be its ultimate king.

Roland de Vaux has written, "Israel is Yahweh's [God's] people and has no other maker but him. That is why from the beginning to the end of its history Israel remained a religious community."

A. Unique Nature. Because Israel's government was given directly by God, it had no true parallel with that of the city-states of the Canaanites, the great empires of later history, or the Greek republic.

Some scholars have tried to parallel Israel's government under Moses and the judges with that of the Greek city-states. From 6 to 12 Greek cities would bind themselves together around a central religious shrine, commit themslves to the same laws, consult together, and cooperate in matters that concerned them all. But the Greeks did not live under God's covenant as Israel did. God made a covenant with Abraham and with His people through Moses, in which He promised that He would be their God and they would be His special people. This made Israel's government radically different in character from any other nation's.

B. Organization. God organized his people into a 12-tribe structure, since He had given Jacob 12 sons (Gen. 49). Other tribes in the Near East organized themselves into units of 12 (cf. Gen. 25:12-16; 36:10-14), but Israel's structure had been mandated by God.

C. Administration. At first, the governmental administration of Israel was very simple. Moses was the God-appointed leader to whom was delegated all authority over God's people. But he soon discovered that there were too many people to rule, and he was busy all day long (Exod. 18:13). Jethro, his father-in-law, suggested that Moses appoint judges to rule over groups of thousands, hundreds, fifties, and tens (Exod. 18:25). With God's approval, Moses chose from among the heads of families. He gave them special instructions and commissioned them to judge the people's everyday problems (Deut. 1:12-18). However, Moses continued to decide the most difficult cases (Exod. 18:26).

The system of government, then, was one of a supreme judge and a court system. The courts settled both religious and civil matters, for in a theocracy no clear-cut line between religious and civil law could exist; all cases were ultimately brought before God (Exod. 18:19).

1. Judicial Responsibilities. The court system also included priests and Levites, who were primarily responsible for directly religious cases, such as murder (Deut. 21:1-9) and rituals for leprosy (Lev. 13–14). The judges also had administrative responsibilities, including oversight of the courts' work (Deut. 19:12; 21; 22:15)

Seal of Shema. This jasper seal (*ca.* eighth century B.C.) discovered at Megiddo is inscribed, "Shema servant of Jeroboam." Seals were used to mark and verify documents and belongings.

and selecting men for warfare (Deut. 20:5-9). Both the judges and the priests were responsible to teach the law to the people (Deut. 17:9; 33:10).

2. Military Responsibilities. The judges had leadership roles; they were appointed as captains over thousands, hundreds, fifties, and tens. It is estimated that there were 78,000 captains in Israel.

THE THEOCRACY IN CANAAN

When the people of Israel conquered the land of Canaan and settled in it, certain changes occurred in their government. They were no longer nomads in the desert; they were now living in cities. They had lost the unity they had while wandering in the wilderness. This transition did not change the structure of Israel's government, but it did change the duties of the judges and the manner of their selection.

The judges became responsible for the government of the towns in which they lived (cf. Num. 21:25, 32; Judg. 8:6, 14, 16). The elders of the tribes had exercised general governmental authority since the days of the Egyptian captivity (cf. Exod. 3:16-18; 19:7); so when they settled in Palestine, some of these elders were elected as judges in the cities (see Judg. 11:5, 11) and sat in the city gates. In other words, they judged civil cases at the city gates, where most civic business was transacted (Ruth 4:1-11).

In cities of refuge, the judges tried persons who were accused of murder (Deut. 19:12). They conducted inquests on people who had died (Deut. 21:2) and settled family and marriage problems (Deut. 21:18; 22:15; 25:7). Families generally settled their own problems according to the decision of the patriarch or family leader, but when there was still dissatisfaction the case would be taken to the judge at the city gates.

Bible scholars believe that Israel's court system included a battery of higher courts in addition to these city judges. Priests sat on the higher courts, to which more difficult cases were referred. However, we have no direct biblical evidence of these higher courts.

During Israel's first settlement of Canaan there was no central authority, king, or ruling body. Each tribe lived in its own area with a minimum of central administration. Since there were few officials, the people had few men to whom to give loyalty and obedience.

After a short period of time, the people of Israel turned from God and began to serve the gods of their Canaanite neighbors. God punished them by sending various nations to oppress them.

However, God loved His people and periodically sent "judges" to deliver them from their oppressors. These men (and one woman) differed from the judges of the court system. They were primarily military leaders rather than judges of the people's dis-

Madame Pharaoh

Ancient governments seldom allowed women to attain positions of leadership. The few women who succeeded in claiming the throne did so by violence or by gradually assuming the powers of a weak male monarch. The first method was used by Athaliah, the only woman to rule Judah, who seized power by murdering her grandsons (2 Kings 11:1-3). The second method was used by Hatshepsut, who slowly assumed the role of pharaoh from her half-brothers.

Hatshepsut (reign 1486–1468 B.C.) was the only surviving child of Pharaoh Thutmose and Ahmose. Ahmose (her mother) was the only descendant of the old Theban princes who had fought and expelled their foreign rulers, the Hyksos. Many Egyptians believed that only the descendants of this line were entitled to rule. In fact, Thutmose had ruled by virtue of his marriage to Ahmose, since the country refused to submit to the rule of a woman.

To provide a pharaoh for the throne when her father died, Hatshepsut married Thutmose II, her step-brother by one of Thutmose's lesser wives. (The Egyptians saw nothing wrong in brother-sister marriages. They felt this made the blood line purer.) But at the time of his coronation, Thutmose II was sickly. He was dominated by his wife, Hatshepsut, and her mother Ahmose. His reign lasted no more than three years.

Thutmose III, another half-brother of Hatshepsut, was then proclaimed pharaoh; but Hatshepsut acted as regent for the young pharaoh. An inscription tells us: "His sister, the Divine Consort, Hatshepsut, adjusted the affairs of the Two Lands

putes. (However, Deborah the prophetess was an exception.

This office was not hereditary, but the Old Testament seems to suggest that the judges came from the ruling class of the people (the elders). Their military leadership lasted only as long as an enemy threatened the borders of Israel (Judg. 8:22-23).

THE UNITED MONARCHY

Israel underweñt a drastic change when theocracy gave way to monarchy (rule by a king). This period of history is usually di-

---

[i.e., Upper and Lower Egypt] by reason of her designs; Egypt was made to labor with bowed head for her, the excellent seed of the god, who came forth from him."

Instead of surrendering her regency when Thutmose came of age, Hatshepsut assumed the titles of the pharaoh. At her temple in Deir el-Bahri, she expended great efforts to make her reign legitimate. Her architect, Senmut, sculptured on the walls a series of reliefs showing the birth of the queen. The god Amon is shown appearing to Ahmose, and he tells her as he leaves: "Hatshepsut shall be the name of this my daughter...She shall exercise the excellent kingship in this whole land." The artist followed court traditions so closely that he pictured Hatshepsut as a boy. The relief shows Hatshepsut's coronation by the gods, and her parents' acknowledgment of her as queen. They represent Thutmose I as saying: "Ye shall proclaim her word, ye shall be united at her command. He who shall do her homage shall live, he who shall speak evil in blasphemy of her majesty shall die."

Hatshepsut's reign brought her greatest prosperity following the collapse of the Middle Kingdom. Extensive building and rebuilding of the temples was carried out under the direction of Senmut. Hatshepsut ordered huge obelisks from the Aswan

quarries, had them inscribed to proclaim the queen, and topped them with gold which reflected the sun so that they could be seen from both sides of the Nile.

Hatshepsut's relations with other nations were peaceful. She was most proud of an expedition to the land of Punt (perhaps modern Somaliland). Five vessels laden with jewelry, tools, and weapons, as well as a great statue of the queen, sailed down the Nile and through a canal connecting the Nile with the Red Sea. When the ships returned, they were loaded "very heavily with the marvels of the country of Punt; all goodly fragrant woods of god's land, heaps of myrrh-resin, of fresh myrrh-trees, with ebony and pure ivory, with the green gold of Emu, with incense, with baboons, monkeys, and dogs....Never was the like of this brought for any king who has been since the beginning."

After Hatshepsut had been pharaoh for 17 years, young Thutmose III brought her reign to an abrupt end. Perhaps because he had waited so long in the background, Thutmose attempted to completely purge the records of her reign. Inscriptions in her temples were chiseled off. Obelisks were sheathed with masonry, covering Hatshepsut's name and the record of their erection. But Thutmose III did not succeed in obliterating Hatshepsut's fame.

vided into two parts, the United Kingdom (*ca.* 1043–930 B.C.) and the Divided Kingdoms (*ca.* 930–586 B.C.). Particularly in the first period, the governmental structure grew more complex.

Israel became a monarchy when Saul was enthroned. The Israelites had been oppressed by the Philistines for many years and wanted to have "a king to judge us like all the nations" (1 Sam. 8:5). They wanted a permanent military leader who would keep them free of other nations' rule. The words "a king to judge" probably emphasize the *military* role that the judges played in the preceding centuries, rather than the judicial role of settling disputes among the people.

A. Choosing a King. The king was chosen by God (1 Sam. 9:15-16), as well as by the people (1 Sam. 11:15). But the people's

Statue of King Khaf-Re. Khaf-Re was a pharaoh of the fourth Egyptian dynasty, about 2700 B.C. The word of the pharaoh was absolute law. The god Horus, depicted as a falcon, extends his wings to cover the king's neck to signify his protection of the monarch. The Israelites did not believe their king was divine.

demand for a king was seen as rejection of God's military leadership; they wanted deliverance from their enemies without obedience to God. Had their attitude toward God been different, God would have provided a king for His people in due course. This event had been planned for centuries before (Deut. 17:14-20). God agreed to their request but predicted judgment against them. Ultimately the king would oppress the people through heavy taxation and by drafting people to work for him and serve in his army (1 Sam. 8:9-18).

B. The Reign of Saul. This prediction began coming true during the reign of Saul. Before he became king, he owned only the usual family property (1 Sam. 9:1-2, 21), but during his reign he distributed fields and vineyards to his officers (1 Sam. 22:7). He must have obtained this property through taxation. At his death he also left considerable property to his heirs (2 Sam. 9:9-10), property which he must have gained during his reign.

Government under King Saul continued to be quite simple, for he did not make any known changes from the previous ways. We know of no administrative or bureaucratic developments during his reign. His only administrators seemed to have been members of his immediate family. His son Jonathan and his cousin Abner served with him in the army and led the militia (1 Sam. 13:1-2, 16; 14:50-51). We also find that Saul established a permanent army in keeping with the desire of the people (1 Sam. 14:52).

C. The Reign of David. During the reign of David, many governmental changes occurred. David led the nation into an era of great military power. He subdued Israel's enemies and dominated over their lands. He had to consolidate the tribes and centralize the government in order to rule the conquered territories and run the government at home.

1. Organization of the Militia. The army was under the command of a general—Joab—and consisted of three sections. One was the original band of about 600 men under 30 commanders (cf. 2 Sam. 23:8-39; 1 Chron. 11:10-47); the other two were the drafted militia and the hired mercenaries. The militia was organized into 12 sections consisting of 24,000 men each. Each section served on active duty for one month a year, and its tribe was responsible to provide for its needs. Probably the elders of the tribes would be the ones who had to see that the support for the militia

Bronze crown. Discovered at Nahal Mishmar in Judea, this bronze crown (*ca.* 3000 B.C.) was a symbol of power and rank. It was worn by an unidentified Canaanite chieftain 1,000 years before the time of Abraham.

was raised (cf. 1 Chron. 27:6-22). It is possible that these men were also responsible for the judicial matters in their tribes.

2. Local Government. David either appointed governors over the people whom he conquered (2 Sam. 8:6, 14) or made their kings his vassals (2 Sam. 10:19). These governors and kings were then responsible to carry on the local government for King David. They had to raise the necessary taxes, tributes, levies, and gifts.

David also appointed men over various treasuries, storehouses, and agricultural enterprises (1 Chron. 26:25-31). The lists of his personal holdings show that the shepherd boy gained many possessions and properties during his reign.

3. Judicial System. As king, David made few changes in the previously existing structure of tribal government. He continued the judicial system established by Moses and allowed cities and tribes to manage their own affairs. The Bible tells us that David used the Levites as civil servants in the court system and the police force of that period (1 Chron. 26:29-32).

4. The King's Cabinet. The king surrounded himself with able men who formed a kind of "cabinet," roughly modeled on the form found in Egypt. These major officials are indicated on pages 83 and 84. Two of the lists of his royal officers are from the early reign of David (2 Sam. 8:15-18; 1 Chron. 18:14-17) while the third is from the end of his reign (2 Sam. 20:23-26).

The office of royal *scribe* or secretary appears frequently throughout the history of the kingdom. (*See* chart on page 85.) This high official seems to have had special assignments from time to time, but his regular duties included writing the royal correspondence and keeping the royal records, the annals of the events during the king's reign (2 Sam. 8:17; 20:25; 1 Chron. 18:16).

The office of *recorder* seems to have been one of high rank from the reign of King David on. He was called *mazkir* in Hebrew ("one who brings to mind"), and his official duty was to advise the king respecting important events. Jehoshaphat, the son of Ahilud, served as recorder for both David and Solomon (2 Sam. 8:16; 1 Kings 4:3). The recorder represented Hezekiah in public business (2 Kings 18:18, 37). During the reign of Josiah the recorder was placed in charge of repairs of the temple (2 Chron. 34:8).

David's cabinet also included several royal counselors or *advisors.* The king trusted these men, who were knowledgeable in many areas; he sought their advice in governing his kingdom. Among David's advisors was Hushai, who is termed the "friend"

David's Cabinet

Title	2 Sam. 8:15-18	1 Chron. 18:14-17	2 Sam. 20:23-36
Recorder	Jehoshaphat, son of Ahilud	Jehoshaphat, son of Ahilud	Jehoshaphat, son of Ahilud
Scribe	Seraiah	Shavsha	Sheva
Priests	Zadok, son of Ahitub Abimelech, son of Abiathar	Zadok, son of Ahitub Abimelech, son of Abiathar	Zadok and Abiathar
Chief Rulers	David's sons	David's sons	Ira the Jairite
"Over the Host" (Army)	Joab, son of Zeruiah	Joab, son of Zeruiah	Joab
"Over the Tribute" (Forced Labor)			Adoram
"Over the Cherethites and Pelethites"	Benaiah, son of Jehoiada	Benaiah, son of Jehoiada	Benaiah, son of Jehoiada

of the king (2 Sam. 15:37); evidently he was a close and respected advisor of David (2 Sam. 16:16; 1 Chron. 27:33). This position was held by only one person at a time. It appeared only under David and Solomon; there is no mention of it in later centuries. In addition to the court official with this title, David's sons were his chief advisors (2 Sam. 8:18; cf. 1 Chron. 18:17). But we do not know the functional relationship between the king's sons and his official advisor.

5. Minor Officials. The Bible mentions a number of minor officials in the king's court during David's reign. One of these was the *saris*, usually translated as "eunuch" (1 Chron. 28:1).

The pharaohs of Egypt had such men, who served as trustees of royal property (Gen. 37:36; 39:1). The neighboring Assyrians had a dignitary called a *sha-reshi*, "he who is at the head," a courtier that may have been a model for the *saris*. The *sha-reshi* was not necessarily a physical eunuch, although he may have been. Scripture indicates that the *saris* of Israel was a trustee much like the Egyptian eunuch or the Assyrian *sha-reshi* (cf. 1 Chron. 28:1; 2 Kings 24:15).

Another official title was "the king's servant" or "the servants of your Lord." This seems to have been a general title that applied

Solomon's Cabinet*

Title	Name
Recorder	Jehoshaphat, son of Ahilud
Scribes	Elihoreph and Ahiah, sons of Shisha
Priests	Zadok and Abiathar; Azaraiah, son of Zadok
"King's Friend"	Zabud, son of Nathan
"Over the Host" (Army)	Benaiah, son of Jehoiada
"Over the Tribute" (Forced Labor)	Adoniram, son of Abda
"Over the Officers"	Azariah, son of Nathan
"Over the Household"	Ahishar

*Based on 1 Kings 4:1-6

to the entire group of officials and royal household servants, from the royal guard to the highest office (1 Kings 1:33; 11:26); in fact, to all those who "stood before" the king (1 Sam. 16:21)—that is, the courtiers in the royal palace (1 Kings 12:6). Sometimes it may have been used as a special title, as in the case of David's uncle, Ahithophel (2 Sam. 15:12).

Finally, there was the *superintendent of forced labor*. This office first appears toward the end of David's reign (2 Sam. 20:24). At first, only non-Israelites were subjected to forced labor (Judg. 1:27-33). Under David foreign people were used extensively for this work, especially in the king's many building projects. The Hebrew word for forced labor or "tribute" is *mas*, and is of Canaanite origin. Perhaps David borrowed the institution from the Canaanites when the need arose.

D. The Reign of Solomon. Under Solomon the administrative structure of government increased greatly. His large standing army, his extremely lavish court, and his many building projects required a complex system of government.

David's son built his government on the foundation of existing structures. First, the elder/judge and the priestly/judge institution continued to be the main government of the cities. The elders con-

Royal Scribes

King	Scribe	Reference
United Monarchy		
David	Seraiah/Shavsha/Sheva	2 Sam. 8:17; 1 Chron. 14:17-18
Solomon	Elihoreph and Ahiah	1 Kings 4:3
Judah		
Jehoash	(Unnamed)	2 Kins 12:10
Uzziah	Jehiel	2 Chron. 26:11
Hezekiah	Shebna	2 Kings 19:2
Josiah, Jehoiakim	Shaphan, Elishama	2 Kings 22:3, 8-10; Jer. 36:10, 12
Zedekiah	Jonathan	Jer. 37:15, 20

tinued to function as they had done under David and for centuries before. Wherever Solomon reorganized the government, he left intact the traditional tribal divisions and loyalties.

1. The King's Cabinet. When we compare the charts on pages 83 and 84, we find many similarities between the cabinets of David and Solomon. Solomon kept David's recorder and the office of royal scribe; in fact, Solomon had two secretaries. Some scholars suggest that he did this because of the increased record-keeping responsibilities during his reign.

The son of David's high priest was the high priest during Solomon's reign. Adoram, David's superintendent of forced labor, also kept his job under Solomon. (He is called Adoniram in 1 Kings 4:6 and 5:14.) The need for forced labor increased during Solomon's reign because of the building of the temple, as well as the construction of palaces and fortifications. Solomon's policy was to fortify and hold the territory that David had conquered. He also had extensive personal properties that required maintenance and needed a large work squad. Solomon began using Israelites as well as non-Israelites in forced labor.

During Solomon's reign the superintendent of forced labor held an important office, for he supervised the work of thousands of people. Adoniram was responsible for 150,000 foreign men in the labor force with 3,600 Israelite supervisors over them. He also had

Royal Viziers

King	Vizier	Reference
	United Monarchy	
Solomon	Ahishar	1 Kings 4:6
	Israel	
Elah	Arza	1 Kings 16:9
Ahab	Obadiah	1 Kings 18:3
Jehoram	(Unnamed)	2 Kings 10:5
	Judah	
Uzziah	Jotham	2 Kings 15:5
Hezekiah	Eliakim	2 Kings 18:18, 37; 19:2

30,000 Israelites working for him, supervised by 300 officers. The entire structure of nearly 184,000 men must have been well organized and carefully policed, but we have no way of knowing exactly how that was done. We do not know whether the army or a special force was responsible to see that the work was done.

Solomon added three new officials to his cabinet: the king's friend, the chief of the prefects, and the official over the royal household. (*See* chart on page 84.)

The king's "friend" functioned much like the advisor of David's cabinet. Zabud held this post under Solomon (1 Kings 4:5).

The chief of the prefects was the cabinet member responsible for all the internal affairs of the kingdom. Under him were the governors or prefects in charge of the 12 districts of the nation created by Solomon. These district governors were responsible for (1) collecting taxes, (2) collecting the temple tithe, (3) supplying the royal court with food for one month each year, (4) lodging soldiers and chariots in the district, (5) erecting public buildings in the district, and (6) constructing and maintaining roads in the district (see 1 Kings 4:7, 21-28).

The office was similar to later administrative offices in the Babylonian Empire. Various nations of the Near East organized their government into 12 districts to provide for the court and army throughout the year (one district per month).

The third new official in King Solomon's structure was the officer over the royal household or *vizier* as he was known in other lands. The chart on page 86 shows that this office continued after Israel split into northern and southern kingdoms.

This official probably was the manager of the king's palace, supervising the maintenance of the grounds, the upkeep of the royal palace, and the assigning of quarters to the court members. He was also responsible for maintaining all royal properties.

Solomon's court was quite lavish when compared to David's. Many people were fed from the king's table. There were about 1,000 administrators and palace officials; Solomon's wives, concubines, and royal children; an unknown number of ambassadors; the entire military complex in the capital, and some of the Levites. The vizier was responsible for feeding all these people; this burden made a great demand on royal revenues. (It is interesting, how-

Reconstruction of Khorsabad. This artist's reconstruction shows the palace of Sargon II (*ca.* eighth century B.C.) at Khorsabad. The size and sumptuousness of the structure attest to the wealth of the Assyrian kings. King Solomon also lived lavishly—but not to this degree.

ever, to note that Solomon's court was much smaller than that of ancient Ebla about 13 centuries before, which included 4,700 bureaucrats.)

The revenue of the palace greatly increased during Solomon's reign, and the vizier had to manage all of these finances. The support of the army and the Levites may have been managed by others. But the vizier was responsible for raising all the funds from the royal estates. Archaeological discoveries suggest that these revenues were used to support the palace courtiers, to supply military needs, and perhaps to provide for the Levites.

Solomon had inherited many estates from his father David, and probably added to these holdings throughout his reign. His lands came through gifts given him (2 Sam. 8:11; 1 Kings 7:51; 15:15), purchases (2 Sam. 24:24; 1 Kings 16:24), conquests and offerings (2 Kings 12:10-11; 22:3-4), and by confiscating the properties of people who had fled the country (2 Kings 8:1-6).

In Israel the king's lands were regarded as being God's lands, since He was the real King of the nation (cf. Lev. 25:23; Deut. 7:6). During Solomon's reign the royal estates, the royal fortresses, and the Levitical cities were closely tied together. The Levites were servants of the kingdom as much as they were servants of the priesthood. This may be why David and Solomon used Levites as civil servants. The kings naturally associated their estates and fortresses with the Levitical lands (Num. 35:1-8). Thus the Levitical lands were also under the vizier's supervision.

The vizier's office can be compared to the Egyptian office of vizier—though under Solomon this official had far less power than his Egyptian counterpart, who was more of a prime minister. He is named toward the bottom of the list of Solomon's court officials (cf. 1 Kings 4:6), and there is no reference to his father.

2. The Queen Mother. Solomon was the first of Israel's kings to include a "queen mother" in his administration—Bath-sheba. She received great honor and sat at his right hand (1 Kings 2:19). Her power was not simply that of a mother over her son; because of her experience, she was considered an important advisor.

A similar office existed among the Hittites and among the people of Ugarit. But in these lands the queen mother often became more active in political affairs.

3. Centralized Government. Solomon's changes in the administrative cabinet served to centralize his government. He structured the district governments in a hierarchy of power, stemming from the power of the king.

Solomon introduced this system sometime during the second half of his reign. Two of the districts were governed by his sons-in-law, Ben-Abinadab and Ahimaaz (1 Kings 4:11, 15). The empire was divided into the following districts:

(1) the house of Joseph
(2-5) former Canaanite territories
(6-7) conquered Transjordan territories
(8-10) the northern tribes
(11) Benjamin
(12) Gad (facing Benjamin on the other side of the Jordan).

These districts are listed in 1 Kings 4:1-19.

Solomon retained most of the old tribal boundaries, only making changes for economic or political reasons. Perhaps his division of districts reflected his suspicion of the northern tribes and was an effort to break up any potentially hostile situations. As a result, districts Three (Sharon and others) and Eleven (Benjamin) gained areas formerly belonging to the house of Joseph, while district One (Joseph) kept the remaining territory. Ephraim and Manasseh had already claimed the Canaanite lands (cf. Judg. 1). So the Transjordan, which had been one administrative district under David, became two districts under Solomon. Solomon may also have made these divisions in order to distribute the tax burden more equally among the 12 tribes.

Solomon's new system eroded the administrative independence of the tribes. He now had a central government, with a local administrative staff appointed by the central government. Israel was no longer a kingdom; it had become an empire.

4. Policy toward the Canaanites. As for the areas where Canaanites still lived, Solomon's policy was to tie them directly to the palace, rather than allowing the Israelite tribes to have jurisdiction over them. Canaanite leaders were given new positions in Solomon's government. With few exceptions, these men were placed over former Canaanite districts (cf. Gen. 10:6-20). These Canaanite prefects or governors were responsible for the collection of taxes and the payment of tribute. Probably Solomon kept the Canaanite districts that had existed during the reign of David (1 Kings 5:1; 10:15).

5. The Central Province. The tribe of Judah does not appear as one of Solomon's 12 districts. Apparently this territory formed a central province, which itself was divided into 12 sections. The Septuagint mentions a "governor of the land" at the end of the list of Solomon's districts. In neighboring Assyria, the term "the land" referred to the central province in their civil administration. In the Assyrian form of government, the central province was not considered part of the overall administrative system of government; it was ruled directly from the palace. Perhaps Solomon's structure followed Assyria's.

E. The Divided Kingdom. The Bible does not tell us very much about the administrative structures of the two divided kingdoms, Israel and Judah. We suppose that the structures of Solomon's time were carried over into both kingdoms.

1. Cabinet Officials. We have some evidence that the kings of

Israel and Judah continued to use the offices of recorder, scribe, vizier, and others. For example, under King Hezekiah the recorder Joah went to negotiate with officials of the invading Assyrian king, Sennacherib (2 Kings 18:18, 27; Isa. 36:3, 22). Another man named Joah was the recorder under King Josiah, and was one of the three officials responsible for repairing the temple (2 Chron. 34:8).

When King Jehoash of Judah rebuilt the temple, he entrusted his scribe and high priest with the control of the money (2 Kings 12:10-11). King Hezekiah sent his scribe Shebna with the elders of the priests and his vizier Eliakim to meet Sennacherib's envoy, and later to confer with the prophet Isaiah (2 Kings 19:2). Under King Josiah, Shaphan the scribe joined Joah the recorder and Maaseiah the governor of the city of Jerusalem in restoring the book of the Law to the temple (2 Chron. 34:8-21).

The office of vizier became more important with the passage of time. In Hezekiah's day, Shebna and his successor Eliakim had great power. Notice how Isaiah describes the office when he predicts that Eliakim will replace Shebna: "And I will clothe him with thy robe, and strengthen him with thy girdle, and I will commit

Judean royal seals. These royal seals were stamped on jar handles in the eighth or seventh centuries B.C. to mark the property of the king. The jar on the top is stamped "Socoh," the one to the bottom reads "Ziph." Some scholars believe royal potteries were located at these cities, and the seal impressions may indicate that the size or volume of the jar was guaranteed by the government.

thy government into his hand: and he shall be a father to the inhabitants of Jerusalem, and to the house of Judah. And the key of the house of David will I lay upon his shoulder; so shall he open, and none shall shut; and he shall shut, and none shall open" (Isa. 22:21-22).

Adoram, the superintendent of forced labor, continued from David's and Solomon's reigns into the time of Rehoboam. In fact, Rehoboam arrogantly sent Adoram to the northern tribes to assert his rule over them; but they showed their contempt for the king of Judah by stoning Adoram (Hadoram) to death (1 Kings 12:18; 2 Chron. 10:18). The office disappeared after the division of the two kingdoms. But in later days Asa forced some men to fortify Geba and Mizpah (1 Kings 15:22) and Jeremiah denounced King Jehoiakim for forcing his people to build his palace (Jer. 22:13).

During the period of the divided kingdom the capital cities—Jerusalem and Samaria—were under a governor as well as the king.

King Darius. This scene from a Grecian vase shows King Darius of Persia (reign 521—485 B.C.) with the symbols of his royal office—the crown, the scepter (in his right hand), and the mace (on his lap). A bodyguard or messenger is giving a report to the king.

In other Near Eastern countries capital cities were administered by a governor. For example, the governor of the central administrative town of Ugarit had authority over the entire surrounding territory.

Scripture mentions "the governor of the city" of Samaria and Jerusalem (1 Kings 22:26; 2 Kings 23:8; 2 Chron. 18:25).

Early in Israel's history Abimelech appointed a governor over Shechem (Judg. 9:29-30). Much later Ahab ordered Amon, the governor of Samaria, to imprison the prophet Micaiah (1 Kings 22:26). In Jehu's day, the governor of Samaria ("he that was over the city"), the vizier ("he that was over the house"), the elders, and the "bringers-up of the children" offered their support and loyalty to him (2 Kings 10:5). Maaseiah administered Jerusalem under King Josiah (2 Chron. 34:8). In Jezebel's plotting to get Naboth's vineyard, she dealt with the elders and the nobles of the city (1 Kings 21:8-11). We have no evidence of governors in the northern kingdom, except for the capital city of Samaria.

Eunuchs were more prominent in the divided monarchy than at previous times. Jeremiah lists them as men of rank with princes and priests (Jer. 34:19). Earlier, such men took Ahab's message to the prophet Micaiah, summoning him to appear before the king (1 Kings 22:9). These "officers" or eunuchs restored the Shunammite's goods (2 Kings 8:6). They were also among those who went into the Babylonian Captivity under Jehoiakim (2 Kings 24:12; Jer. 29:2), having led the men of Israel in fighting against the Babylonians at the capture of Jerusalem (2 Kings 25:19; Jer. 52:25).

2. Queen Mothers. We find mention of two queen mothers in the divided kingdom, Maakah misused her office and was deposed by King Asa (1 Kings 15:13), and Athaliah later took control of the nation (2 Kings 11:1-16).

3. Minor Officials. In light of the Scripture evidence that cabinet offices continued into this period, we may safely assume that priest administrators, military heads, administrators over local districts, and other minor officials continued in each kingdom.

A new minor official who appears in the divided monarchy is the "king's son." He appears to have been some kind of policeman and did not hold high rank in the governmental structure (cf. 1 Kings 22:26-27; 2 Chron. 18:25). Perhaps the title indicates that a king's son originally held this office.

SUMMARY

The government of the nation of Israel began with a theocracy in the wilderness where Israel was a religious community ruled by God with a system of tribal courts. Moses was chief executive over a staff of judges who gave decisions in disputes and apparently served as leaders in battle.

The theocracy in Canaan remained simple, with its civil government centered in the cities where elder-judges settled disputes. Later God raised up another type of judge to deliver the Israelites from their oppressors.

The monarchy in Israel became centralized and more complex. The rule by kings Saul, David, and Solomon eventually resulted in division of the nation.

Local administration in the divided kingdoms was adjusted from time to time by various reforms and changes of government. But the elders (or judges) still continued as the primary government officials responsible for the judicial processes and local civil needs. This best explains how the returning exiles were able to assume so quickly a form of government that was patterned after the pre-kingdom administrative structure.

6

LAWS AND STATUTES

God told Moses how the people of Israel should live, and Moses recorded these commands in the first 5 books (the *Pentateuch*) of the Old Testament. These laws teach us a great deal about Old Testament society; but they also suggest how our own society should work. God still expects His people to honor Him in their dealings with one another. The laws of the Old Testament teach us to lift up God and respect the rights of our neighbors. As interpreted by Jesus and His apostles, they form the foundation of modern Christian ethics.

UNIQUENESS OF BIBLICAL LAW

Since the legal system of the Bible helped to shape that of the West today, it does not seem strange to us. But we can discern the uniqueness of biblical law when we compare it with other ancient systems of law. Archaeologists have found collections of Near Eastern laws in the ruins of Ur-Nammu, Eshnunna, Sumer, Mari, Ugarit, and other cities.

King Hammurabi of Babylon produced a famous system of law around 1700 B.C. The Hittites of Asia Minor adopted similar ideas when they created their own well-known legal system. The Sumerians, the Babylonians, the Assyrians, and other peoples of Mesopotamia greatly influenced the laws of the world around them. S. M. Paul says that nearly every legal system of the ancient Near East "bore the imprint of Mesopotamia."

The various law-codes of Mesopotamia followed the same general pattern: instead of giving universal guidelines, they stated what had been traditionally decided in a series of actual court cases. In other words, Mesopotamian law was *case law*. (Scholars often call it *casuistic* law—a term which comes from the Latin word *casus*, meaning "case.") The people of the Near East believed their king could apply eternal truth to every new problem. After all, hadn't the gods chosen him to rule them? So when he made a judgment, he bound all of his people to it, and they did not demur. However, later kings just quoted tradition and did little to codify or modify law in terms of life situations.

Mesopotamian laws told people how to handle their money and property, how to collect damages, how to get a divorce, and so on, but did not teach moral or religious lessons.

A code of Mesopotamian law usually opened by telling how gods gave the king power to rule the land. Then the book listed the rulings on a series of legal cases, arranged by topic. It closed with curses for anyone who disobeyed the king's laws and blessings for those who kept them. (There are sections of the Pentateuch that list God's rulings according to this pattern.)

Mesopotamian legal codes begin each rule by saying, "Thus you shall do." Often a biblical commandment begins with the words, "Thus saith the LORD." But notice the difference: In the Bible, God gives the command; in Mesopotamian law, the king does.

The content of biblical law often resembles other laws of the Near East. But in many more ways, biblical law is different. Biblical law codes are unique in their form, their origin, their concept of law, and their underlying principles.

A. The Form of the Law. As we have noted, most law systems of the Near East consisted of case laws; they laid out the age-old traditional decisions in various legal cases. They were cold, hard, and capricious. But the laws of the Bible point back to a personal lawgiver: God.

The Bible says that God gave His Law with a purpose of love. Though the laws of the Bible are firm, they point to a God who cares about human beings personally, and therefore direct how they should live so as to please Him and enjoy His favor. Bible scholars call this the *apodictic* form of law, because it demonstrates how God governs His people. (*Apodictic* comes from the Greek word *apodeiktikos*, which means "demonstrative.") In Mesopotamia it was the king's *word* that was binding; his decree in a specific case was the law. When his word was written, everyone had to obey it—even the king himself (cf. Esther 8:8; Dan. 6:12). But the law of God was different. God's statements did not control Israel; God did. He was free to act on His own initiative and He chose to act according to His own righteous character, and obedience to His

Code of Hammurabi. An early king of Babylon (eighteenth century B.C.), Hammurabi set up one of the earliest known legal codes. He improved upon earlier codes and had the laws recorded on a stone stele, set up in the temple of Marduk at Babylon where the people could see it. Discovered at Susa, the Code of Hammurabi is the longest and the most complete legal document ever found in the Near East. It contains over 280 laws.

law was a direct expression of love and loyalty to God Himself. This is why biblical law contains so much moral and religious material: it tells about God and His relationship with His people.

Most of God's commandments were meant to last for centuries, but occasionally He gave short-term instructions. When the Israelites entered Canaan, for example, He told them to destroy the pagan shrines (Deut. 12:2), to set up a civil court system (Deut. 16:8), and to establish cities of refuge (Deut. 19:1-13). These short-term commands revealed God's love under the temporary conditions of conquest.

The Bible may express God's Law in the form of general statements of policy or as rulings for specific cases (cf. Exod. 21:16; Deut. 24:7). Sometimes both forms (general and specific, apodictic law and case law) appear side-by-side in the same text. The Bible doesn't use one legal form as the Mesopotamian law systems do. Because God spoke to His people in many different situations, His commands appeared in various forms.

B. The Origin of the Law. Rulers of the Near East were not trying to express universal wisdom through their laws. They were trying to maintain their personal political and economic power and their image as lawgivers. If a previous king had already done this they just borrowed the ideas for their own legal system. A king was supposed to hand down laws that were clear, just, and true, no matter where he got them.

In contrast, the Bible teaches that God's people received their laws from God Himself, not from their neighbors. Even laws

Babylonia contract. This contract from the seventeenth century B.C. records the division of an inheritance among several heirs. It bears 25 impressions made by 7 different seals that belonged to the contracting parties and witnesses.

whose content corresponded to those of other Near Eastern codes are presented as God-given. The Bible says to obey its laws because they are God's commands. Such a statement is called a *motive clause*, because it blesses those who obey God's Law and curses those who disobey it, or both (e.g., Lev. 26). The opening chapters of Deuteronomy (1–4) review Israel's history with a motivating purpose, to remind God's people that they ought to obey His laws. The Israelites agreed with their neighbors that the law was eternal and binding, but for a different reason—not because the king said so, but because God said so.

C. The Concept of Law. Laws usually deal with a nation's social order; they tell how citizens should act toward one another. But the laws of the Bible also tell how God's people should act toward Him. Indeed, they are primarily religious laws.

God introduces His Law by saying that He chose Israel to be a nation with its own land, not just a clan or a large family (see Gen. 12:2). God's Law then told the people of Israel how to live in harmony with Him. This was the message of the Ten Commandments or *Decalogue* ("ten words," Exod. 20), and the thrust of the civil laws in the legal section of Exodus (chs. 21–23) as well as the rules of worship (Exod. 24–31). Man served God and His Law; man did not make the law.

Hittite law assumed that a god was the *suzerain* (conquering ruler) of the nation. But in the Bible, the relationship between God and Israel is a more personal one. Israel is God's "treasured possession" (cf. Exod. 19:3-6).

Biblical law was public law, and this was another important difference from the pagan laws of the Near East. In many nations of the ancient Near East, the king carried the laws in his head, as if they were his personal possession. He did not publish them until he was ready to give up his throne. Thus a person could be arrested for breaking a law he had never known. The laws were kept secret, even when a person was put on trial for breaking them. (There are few instances in which anyone cited the royal codes in a court case.)

But in Israel, the leaders of government read God's Law to the people at regular times of the year (cf. Deut. 31:10-13). Thus every citizen could learn the laws he had to obey. Other peoples of the Near East obeyed laws because they were enforced by the royal

Brotherly pact. This stele from Ras-Shamra (*ca.* fourteenth century B.C.) shows two men standing on opposite sides of a table with their hands extended to touch. This act probably marked the formalizing of a pact between the two parties. Genesis 31:44-53 tells how Laban and Jacob made a similar covenant.

establishment; disobedience meant punishment. But God's people were to obey His Law because they loved Him (cf. Deut. 6:5, 20-25).

In Israel, the claim of the law rested on the known character of the Lawgiver. Even though the judges and priests interpreted the law, they did not make the law (Deut. 17:8-13). So when people abided by the law, they showed their love for God, rather than for His interpreters.

D. Underlying Principles. The principles that stood behind the laws of the Bible are in marked contrast to those behind other Near Eastern laws. We have noted that the laws of the Bible were based upon the revealed character and purpose of God Himself. Rather than being the political whim of a human king or the mere traditions of the state, the Bible's laws point toward a transcendant goal—God's redemption of mankind. They show God's protection of each individual's integrity. They reflect the fact that God made man a steward of the earth (Deut. 21:22-23).

We see another fundamental difference in the social distinctions embodied in ancient Near Eastern codes. The Code of Hammurabi, for example, preserves 3 separate social classes and codifies the degradation of the lower class. It is a system designed to protect the position of the few people at the top of society. Biblical law sees all men as the creatures of God, equal to one another. Other important themes emerge as we study biblical Law.

1. All Crimes Ultimately Crimes against God. God built Israelite society on His own rules; so when a person offended society, he thereby offended God (1 Sam. 12:9-10). In fact, some social offenses were so serious that only God could pardon them.

2. Total Submission to God. God's laws showed that He cares about every aspect of a person's life. It was not enough to give Him formal worship or moral behavior. Since each person's whole being came from God, God expected all His people to serve Him with their whole being (Amos 5:21-24).

God enforced His Law when His human agents would not (Exod. 22:21-24; Deut. 10:18; Psa. 67:4). He undertook to punish His people when they did not apply His Law fairly. He was present as Judge at every court trial, no matter what verdict the human judge rendered (cf. Deut. 19:17).

3. National Responsibility. As we have seen, God's Law wasn't the private property of the upper class; each person knew

Bust of Hammurabi. This diorite head discovered at Susa dates from the eighteenth century B.C. Many researchers believe it represents Hammurabi, who welded the small states of Babylonia into a single powerful kingdom. In addition to his well-known legislative abilities, Hammurabi was a military genius and a man of literary talent.

the law and the penalty for breaking it. Often the whole community punished the lawbreaker, because all of the people had to uphold the law (Exod. 21:22-23).

Judges represented God, but they also represented the law-abiding community. Executioners meted out punishment on behalf of the total community. Thus a murder case required evidence from 2 or 3 witnesses, and the verdict was announced publicly at the city gate. Sometimes the witnesses executed a murderer (Deut. 13:6-10; 17:7). Sometimes the victim's next of kin did it (Deut. 19:11-12), and sometimes the whole community took part (Num. 15:32-36; Deut. 13:6-10).

4. Individual Responsibility. The Bible stresses that each person's duty to God was more important than the duty to go along with his community. If his community was wrong, God still held him responsible for his own actions (cf. Exod. 32).

5. Respect for Human Life. Since man was created in God's image, God's Law protected human life. If someone injured a person of lower social status, he was not excused by the mere payment of a fine. The only equivalent of human life was human life itself. God said that every murderer should be executed (Gen. 9:6).

Laws Concerning a Goring Ox

Code of Eshnunna (Old Babylonian—ca. 2000 B.C.)	Code of Hammurabi (Babylonian—ca. 1700 B.C.)	The Pentateuch (Hebrew—ca. 1440 B.C.)
54—If an ox is known to gore habitually and the authorities have brought the face to the knowledge of its owner, but he does not have his ox dehorned, it gores a man and causes [his] death, then the owner of the ox shall pay two-thirds of a mina of silver.	251—If a man's ox was a gorer and his city council made it known to him that it was a gorer, but he did not pad its horns [or] tie up his ox, and that ox gored a member of the aristocracy, he shall give one-half mina of silver.	Exodus 21:29 (RSV)— But if the ox has been accustomed to gore in the past, and its owner has been warned but has not kept it in, and it kills a man or a woman, the ox shall be stoned, and its owner also shall be put to death.
55—If it gores a slave and causes [his] death, he shall pay 15 shekels of silver.	252—If it was a man's slave, he shall give one-third mina of silver.	Exodus 21:32 (RSV)— If the ox gores a slave, male or female, the owner shall give to their master thirty shekels of silver, and the ox shall be stoned.

6. Equitable Penalties. Other laws of the Near East allowed a victim to inflict more injury than he had received. They also allowed some criminals to pay back less than they had stolen or less than the injury they had caused. God ruled that the courts could only require "eye for eye, tooth for tooth" (Exod. 21:24), which made the law more equitable. This is often called "the law of the claw" (Latin, *lex talionis*).

7. Personal Punishment. Outside Israel, rich people could buy their way out of punishment; but God declared that every lawbreaker must suffer for his own crime. If a judge was too easy on the lawbreaker, he became guilty of the crime too. No one could pay a ransom for the criminal (Num. 35:31)—except that when an animal committed an offense, its owner could buy it back (Exod. 21:29-30). Only the system of religious sacrifice allowed a person to offer a substitute for punishment.

8. Universal Justice. God's Law protected the rights of the poor, the widow, the orphan, and the alien. God ruled that no Israelite could be enslaved forever (Exod. 21:2) and He guarded slaves from abuse (Exod. 21:20-21, 26-27), including foreigners who were enslaved (Lev. 25:44). He forbade heavy penalties for debt, and He told His people to share their goods with the needy.

E. A Case Comparison. Let's look at one specific example of how biblical law compares with other laws of the ancient Near East. We will compare what the different laws said about a "goring ox." (See chart on page 102.) Notice that the law of the Bible:

—Placed greater value on human life than on animal life.

—Valued the life of a woman as much as the life of a man.

—Valued the life of a child as much as the life of an adult.

—Found the ox guilty of murder.

—Upheld the rule of "a life for a life."

—Condemned a careless owner to die along with his ox.

—Applied the *lex talionis* with mercy, putting the blame on the guilty party alone.

—Set a higher value on human life. (It may be worth all that a man has.)

—Recognized that a slave was still a human being.

—Restored a slave's services to his master. (It requires the ox's owner to pay him 30 shekels, the purchase price of a slave.)

—Put no price on a normal citizen. (Because he was God's servant, he was beyond price.)

—Allowed the community to decide the price of justice, instead of setting a stated fine for every case.

BODIES OF OLD TESTAMENT LAW

It's interesting to compare the various collections of Old Testament laws: the Book of the Covenant (Exod. 20:22–23:33), the Deuteronomic Code (Deut. 12–26), and the Holiness Code (Lev. 17–27).

A. The Book of the Covenant. Technically, the "Book of the Covenant" was everything that Moses read to the Israelites at the foot of Mount Sinai (cf. Exod. 24:3-7), including the Ten Commandments (Exod. 20:2-17). Later Jewish leaders called the Book of Deuteronomy the "Book of the Covenant" (2 Kings 21:2; 23:2; 2 Chron. 34:30). Deuteronomy is generally thought to be "the book of the law" discovered during the restoration of the temple under King Josiah of Judah (2 Kings 22:8).

The Israelites accepted the entire law as part of their covenant with God. They believed that the Decalogue stated the basic rules of the law, while the other Old Testament laws applied these principles and clarified them. This is why both the Ten Commandments with the detailed Sinai Legislation, and equally the entire Book of Deuteronomy, in which the Sinai Legislation is reapplied and amplified, may be called the "Book of the Covenant."

B. The Holiness Code. God unfolded His laws over a span of many generations. The Ten Commandments were expanded and explained in Exodus 20:22–23:33. In turn, the laws of Leviticus and Deuteronomy expanded and explained the laws of Exodus. Leviticus explained the first 4 commandments of the Decalogue—those that had to do with the worship of God—while most of Deuteronomy dealt with the rest of the Decalogue.

The collection of laws found in Leviticus 17–26 is called the Holiness Code; its primary concern was to keep Israel—God's chosen people—holy and pure. The purpose of the Holiness Code was clearly expressed in Leviticus 20:26: "And ye shall be holy unto me: for I the LORD am holy, and have severed you from other people, that ye should be mine."

C. The Deuteronomic Code. Bible scholars disagree about how much of the Book of Deuteronomy makes up the Deuteronomic Code. (Some believe that Deuteronomy 1–11 continues the discussion of worship from the Book of Leviticus; others include this section in the Holiness Code, because it differs from the rest of the Book of Deuteronomy.)

But the Decalogue (Deut. 5) laid the foundation for the Book of Deuteronomy. The laws that governed human relationships would have made no sense without the laws governing man's relationship with God. So it is more logical to see the Book of Deuteronomy as a complete work, and to call the entire book the "Deuteronomic Code." It covers the wide range of ethical and ritual concerns that Moses raised with the Israelites just before they entered the Promised Land.

Notice that the Book of Exodus divides its case laws from its gen-

Sinai. The mountain slope on the left is Jebel Musa, the traditional Mount Sinai. Moses climbed the rugged face of Sinai to receive from God the set of laws now known as the Ten Commandments. These laws became the core of all biblical law.

eral legal policies (Exod. 21:1–22:17; 22:18–23:33). The fact that Deuteronomy blends these two forms of law together confirms that it was probably written later. Also notice that the laws of Deuteronomy were designed for a more settled way of life; for instance, the book adds laws of inheritance (Deut. 21:15-17) and interest on loans (Deut. 23:20) to the Exodus laws. These new laws reflected a life that would be less nomadic. When Deuteronomy was written, the Israelites were no longer destined to wander in the wilderness; they were ready to conquer Canaan and settle

The Mezuzah

When the angel of death passed over Egypt, killing all firstborn males, Jewish families were protected by the blood of the paschal lamb on the doorposts of their homes (Exod. 12:23). Today many Jews attach a *mezuzah* to their doorposts as a reminder of God's presence and the Jewish people's redemption from Egypt.

The *mezuzah* (Hebrew, "doorpost") is a small case containing a parchment on which the following prayer is written: "Hear, O Israel, the Lord our God, the Lord is One. And thou shalt love the Lord thy God with all thy heart, and with all thy soul, and with all thy might. And these words which I command thee this day shall be upon thy heart. Thou shalt teach them diligently unto thy children, and shalt speak of them when thou sittest in thy house, when thou walkest by the way, when thou liest down and when thou riseth up. And thou shalt bind them for a sign upon thy hand and they shall be for frontlets between thine eyes. And thou shalt write them upon the doorposts of thy house and upon thy gates" (Deut. 6:4-9).

The parchment continues with Deuteronomy 11:13-21, which emphasizes obedience to the commandments and the rewards of a righteous life.

Even today each mezuzah parchment is carefully written by qualified scribes, using the same strict procedures they use in writing the laws. It is then tightly rolled and placed in its case so that the word *shaddai* ("Almighty") appears through a small hole near the top. A special prayer is read when the mezuzah is attached near the top of the right-hand doorpost. Though the popularity of the mezuzah has diminished in recent years, many Jews still kiss the mezuzah by touching their lips with their fingers and raising the fingers to a mezuzah when entering or leaving the home. At the same time, they recite Psalm 121:8: "The Lord shall preserve thy going out and thy coming in from this time forth, and even forevermore."

The mezuzah is a Jewish family's daily reminder of their responsibility to God and their community. It is a sign to the community that this home is one where the laws of God reign supreme. Within this sanctuary, away from worldly influences, the Jewish family studies the Scripture, observes religious holidays, and instructs their children in the faith of their fathers.

An ancient Hebrew scholar explained the purpose of the mezuzah by comparing it to the guards of an earthly king. In the same way that a king has guards at the gate to assure him of his security, the people of Israel are safe within their homes because the Word of God is at the door to guard them.

down. We find more of these domestic laws in the Book of Numbers, such as the laws of a woman's inheritance (Num. 27:1-11; 36:1-12).

FUNCTIONAL DEVELOPMENT OF LAW

The law of Israel developed over several hundred years as God gave each generation the instructions it needed for its way of life. When the laws of the Bible are grouped by topic, we get a picture of how they unfolded through the centuries.

A. Ceremonial Law. The ancient Israelites centered all of their activities on the worship of Jehovah. Each person was expected to worship God individually, just as the whole nation was to worship Him together. Jesus recalled this when He said He could sum up all the commands of the Old Testament in one commandment—to love God (Matt. 22:37; cf. Deut. 6:5; Lev. 19:18).

In great detail, the Bible described the ceremonies of worship that were so important to the life of God's people. These scriptures show that even though a person cannot please God on his own, God makes that person able to worship Him acceptably.

1. Ark of the Covenant. The Bible's ceremonial law mentioned several sacred objects that the Israelites kept at the center of their camp as they wandered in the wilderness. The most important of these was the ark of the covenant.

The ark of the covenant was a wooden box about 122 x 76 x 76 cm. (4 x 2½ x 2½ ft.), or 2½ x 1½ cubits. It was made of acacia ("*shittim*," KJV) wood and covered with gold, inside and out. The Israelites believed this box was God's throne, and so they called its solid gold lid the "mercy seat." Two golden cherubim (angelic statues) stood on opposite ends of the box, facing the mercy seat (Exod. 25:10-22). Inside the box the Israelites kept the stone tablets on which God gave them the Ten Commandments, a pot of manna, and Aaron's rod—all reminders of God's love for them.

The Israelites carried this ark at the head of their procession across the Jordan River (Josh. 3-4). Arabian tribes carried similar arks into battle as a magic charm to gain their gods' favor. But the ark of the covenant was a symbol of the covenant between God and men, not a magic charm.

2. Central Sanctuary. God promised Israel that some day they would be at "rest" in a land of their own (cf. Heb. 4). When that day came, they were supposed to build a central sanctuary where they could worship Him.

God chose all of the Israelites to be His priests (Exod. 19:6), but most of them had to earn a living. Therefore He ordered that the tribe of Levi should represent the whole nation in the sanctuary (Exod. 28:43–29:9). The Levites had to follow special rules to keep themselves pure for this kind of service. God chose the Levitical family of Aaron to be His priests, and they had to follow stricter rules (Lev. 10:8-11). From them, God chose one man to be the high prest and gave him even more special rules.

Why God would lay out such complex rules for worship puzzles many modern readers of the Bible. But the crucial idea behind the ceremonial laws was *holiness*, that is, separation, closeness, and conformity to God. Obedience to the laws assured that God's people would be different from all others. The worship of God was most important in their lives, so they devoted much time and care to it.

B. Dietary Law. God gave the Israelites a special diet to emphasize that they were His special people (Deut. 12:15). He did not allow them to eat meat that was improperly butchered (Lev. 7:22-27) or any of the first fruits from a plant (Exod. 23:19; 34:26). He gave them many other rules about their diet. Here are some examples:

—They could not eat any blood, because life was in the blood (Deut. 12:23) and it was a covering (atonement) for sin (Lev. 17:11).

—They could not eat any animal fat, because it should be offered to God (Lev. 7:23, 31).

—They could not eat animals killed by wild beasts or animals that died of natural causes (Lev. 7:22-27).

—They could not eat scavenger animals, such as vultures (Deut. 14:11-20), or organs that remove impurities from an animal's body (Exod. 29:13, 22).

—They could eat water animals with scales or fins, but not others, such as the otter (Deut. 14:9-10).

—They could eat any plant-eating animals which both chewed their cud and had a parted hoof (such as cows), but not others (Deut. 14:6-8).

—They could not eat any crawling or flying insects, except those of the locust and beetle families (Lev. 11:22-23).

—They could eat any fruits after the fourth harvest (Lev. 19:23), as well as any vegetables and grains (Gen. 1:29-30) or eggs (Deut. 22:6-7).

—They could not eat or drink anything that had been left open in a room with a dead or dying person (Num. 19:11-22).

—They could not eat a goat's kid boiled in its mother's milk because this was a pagan ritual of the Canaanites (Exod. 23:19).

Some basic concepts of biblical law emerge from this list. First, God's people were to give Him what was rightfully His (the blood and fat). Second, they were to avoid contact with sources of defilement, such as the dead. Third, they were to avoid anything pagan or idolatrous. Fourth, all of the dietary laws came from God; He alone decided what His people should eat.

C. Quarantine Law. God laid down strict rules about death, illness, childbirth, and a woman's monthly menstrual period. The Israelites learned that these things could make them unclean and unfit for acceptable worship (cf. Lev. 12; 14:1-32; 15).

The Israelites knew that God was a God of the living, so they accepted that they must keep death away from their worship. If they touched a corpse, they could not go to a worship service until they had cleansed themselves (Lev. 22:3-7).

God blessed marriage and the raising of a family (Deut. 28:11), but His laws on childbirth reminded the Israelites that they were born in sin. (A woman who bore a child had to cleanse herself by rituals; so did the midwife and anyone else who attended the birth—Lev. 12.) These laws also reminded the Israelites that sex was not a part of their worship. This set them farther apart from other ancient cultures, for whom fertility rites and temple prostitutes formed an important part of worship.

D. Laws of Dedication. God taught the Israelites that the firstborn of every family, animal, and plant belonged to Him. They gave the firstborn to God as a symbol of giving all life back to Him. Because God counted Israel His firstborn among mankind, He called the nation to dedicate itself to serving Him (Exod. 4:22-23).

God claimed the Israelites as His people when they lived in Egypt. Answering His call, they followed Moses into the wilderness and entered into a *covenant* (a treaty or agreement) with God at Mount Sinai. They agreed to let the tribe of Levi represent the firstborn of the nation in its worship ceremony (Num. 3:40-41; 8:18). The other Israelites paid a fee to excuse their own firstborn children from this duty (Lev. 27:1-8). Once a year they sacrificed the firstborn of all flocks, herds, and fields to the Lord (Deut. 14:22-27). After the Israelites settled in Canaan, God told them to give these first-fruits to the Levites (Lev. 23:10, 17). This demonstrated that the land and all its fruits belonged to God.

The Israelites probably gave three tithes. They called the first "the Lord's tithe." It was one-tenth of their money and produce, and they gave it to the Levites, who weren't allowed to own any land (Num 18:21-24). From what they received, the Levites gave a tithe to the priests (Num. 18:26).

The Israelites gave a second tithe three times a year when they went to the central sanctuary (Deut. 12:6-7, 17-18). They gave the third tithe once every three years; they left it at the city gate to be distributed among the Levites, strangers, orphans, and widows (Deut. 14:27-29). These tithes amounted to about 13 percent of a man's total income.[1] The tithe system allowed all of the Israelites to offer their possessions to God. It spread the responsibility for maintaining worship among the rich and the poor, the willing and the unwilling. God ordered the Israelites not to plant their land in the seventh year (Exod. 23:10-11), and He did not require a tithe in that year. Thus God expected men to recognize His Lordship, but He demanded only a relatively small portion of their property for Himself.

In addition to these tithes, every adult male of the wilderness generation paid a poll tax to raise funds for constructing the tabernacle (Exod. 38:24-31). All Israelite men over the age of 20 paid this tax.

E. Laws of Religious Symbolism. God commanded the Israelites to wear certain symbols to show their dedication to Him. For example, Jewish men wore *phylacteries*—tiny containers that held key Bible texts. The Old Testament often mentions the phylacteries, but gives no specific command from God concerning them (Exod. 13:9; Deut. 6:8; 11:18). An Israelite would tie the phylactery to his forehead, his left hand, or the doorpost of his house.

God told the Israelites to wear blue fringes on their garments

(Deut. 22:12; Num 15:37-41). These fringes showed a person's commitment to God's royal law. Jesus wore them (Matt. 9:20), but He condemned Jews who made their fringes large to boast of their dedication to God (Matt. 23:5).

F. Civil Law. The people of Israel knew themselves called to worship God with their entire lives. This meant that their obedience extended to the realm of civil laws as well as of religious laws. They consulted God when they selected their leaders, and they looked to God to guide their government. They believed that God had set up the powers of civil government for their own good.

1. Political Leaders. God would not allow anyone who had a physical handicap to serve in a position of leadership. He banned from office any male who was sexually maimed, anyone who was born out of wedlock, and anyone who was a Moabite or Ammonite (mixed races). The law prevented these people from entering the "congregation of the LORD," the chief political body of the nation (Deut. 23:1-3).

These laws offend our modern sense of democracy, but we must remember that ancient Israel was not a democracy. It was a *theocracy* (a government ruled by God), and God stressed that His people should be pure. He wanted Israelites to be spiritually clean and perfect; He symbolized this by allowing only those who were physically and racially perfect to come into His presence.

God gave Israel specific instructions for choosing a king (Deut. 17:14-20). Some modern scholars believe that these laws date from after the time of Moses, but there is no proof of that. What is said is that God required a king who would submit to the laws of the covenant, and this is fully in keeping with the teachings of the rest of the Pentateuch.

Anticipating the Israelites' desire for a king, God laid down the laws of Deuteronomy to make sure that the king would not lead the people away to paganism. But the Israelites did not need these laws until many generations after Moses (cf. 1 Sam. 8:5).

2. Israel's Army. God allowed Israel to raise an army for defense (Num. 2:14), but He did not want His people to become a war-like nation, greedy for land and power. He would not let them have war horses (Deut. 17:16), nor would He let them keep anything they captured in war. But they could protect the borders of the Promised Land from any invaders, and they could crush rebel

armies within their country. The generals of Israel could draft soldiers from the men over 20 years of age (cf. Num. 1:21-43), except
for the Levites (Num. 1:48-49). God promised to help the army of
Israel if the soldiers obeyed His laws (Deut. 23:9-14). Israel must
try to make peace with its enemies before going into battle, but often Israel had to destroy its enemies (Deut. 2:34; 3:6). Sometimes
God allowed the troops to spare young virgins and marry them.
But if a soldier decided to do this, he could not treat the woman as
a slave or captive (Deut. 21:10-14). Even in war, God told the Israelites to respect the life He had created. He ordered them to protect all innocent forms of life, including the fruit trees (Deut.
20:19-20).

3. The Court System. Israel had a dual system of courts. The
nation elected judges to hear civil law suits, while the Levites
judged religious matters (cf. Deut. 17:8-13; 2 Chron. 19:8, 11).
Each court system had several layers of lesser courts (cf. Deut.
1:15-16). The judges heard cases of all kinds and taught the laws to
the people (Deut. 17:11; 2 Chron. 17:7-9).

The law required witnesses to tell the truth or suffer the same
penalty ås the accused one (Exod. 23:1-3). Two or three witnesses
had to give consonant testimony in order to convict a person of a
serious crime. A person could not be convicted on the basis of only
one witness' testimony (Deut. 17:6). Anyone who refused to ac-
cept the verdict of the court could be put to death (Deut. 17:12-
13).

The courts had room for mercy, though. If someone committed
murder by accident, he could go to a city of refuge—i.e., a city
where he could live without being punished (Deut. 19:1-14). But
the fugitive could enter the city only if he convinced the city's
judges that the killing was indeed an accident. The Bible set up
these cities of refuge to protect the lives of innocent people. (Anyone who fled to a city of refuge could go free when the high priest
died.) The judges controlled these cities, which were an important
feature of Israel's civil law.

G. Criminal Law. The criminal laws of Israel can be divided
into several categories. Of course, all crimes were serious because
they were sins against God. But some crimes were more destructive, and they carried a heavier penalty.

1. Crimes against Religion. Some crimes offended God directly, dishonoring Him by evil speech and rebellious action. A person might reject God and the life He offers; he might worship a pagan God, betray the people of God, or abuse the holy rituals of worship. If so, he would be put to death. In some cases, his own relatives would execute him (Deut. 13:6-9). When such a case came to trial, the judges investigated it very carefully. They cross-examined the witnesses and checked the evidence several times. If a witness gave false testimony on a matter of such importance, he was put to death.

The Bible listed several crimes of this type. Among them were child sacrifice (a form of murder), sorcery, and violation of the Sabbath. (The Sabbath law was strict because the Sabbath symbolized God's promise of eternal rest.)

Samaritan scroll of the Law. Inhabitants of northern Israel, the Samaritans reject all Old Testament Scripture except the Pentateuch. The Samaritans intermarried with foreign tribes after the restoration to Israel in the fifth century B.C., which created the ancient antipathy between the Samaritans and the Jews.

2. Crimes against Society. Anyone who tried to bribe a judge or give false testimony was found guilty of a crime against society (Exod. 23:1-7; Deut. 19:16-21); for he was trying to injure the person on trial and undercut God's system of justice. This kind of crime was both a civil and religious offense.

God's Law did not allow judges to torture witnesses or to take bribes. They were required to treat all defendants with equity (Deut. 16:18-19). As the law respected a witness so it required much of him. It forced him to pay the price of death for lying (Deut. 19:16-21). The law also gave death to a son who cursed or struck his parents (Exod. 21:15, 17), because he was attacking the family, the foundation of his society. By the same token, it protected the son from evil parents because it did not permit child abuse.

The criminal law of the Old Testament affirms that God controls life. He creates life, and only He can decide to cut it off. The death penalty protected law-abiding citizens from any evil person who might want to seize power in their community.

It protected the family and the individual, too. A rebellious son who struck his parents was to be executed in the public marketplace as a lesson to other children (Exod. 21:18-21). God expected His people to raise their children so that they would respect the law. But in the end, each child was responsible for what he did.

3. Crimes against Morality. The laws of the Bible form a unique moral system. While other laws of the Near East tried to show what a king thought was good and right, the Bible shows how to honor God; this theme runs through all of its laws and is the root of all its morality.

The Bible outlaws adultery, unnatural sex acts (such as homosexuality), prostitution, and other forms of perverted sex. God knew that these things could destroy Israel, just as they had destroyed other nations. They were crimes against morality—in other words, crimes challenging the God-given order for human society.

God's Law ruled out greed, lying, strange marriages, and anything else that would upset society. God expected His people to live morally upright lives.

4. Crimes against the Person. These crimes included murder, abortion, rape, and kidnapping. Each carried the death penalty.

Let us take a close look at the law concerning rape, because it sheds light on the Bible's understanding of woman.

If a woman was attacked and did not cry out for help, her attacker was not guilty of rape. But if she sought help without being able to get it and if she was married or betrothed, her attacker was put to death. If an unmarried woman was raped, the attacker had to pay a dowry price (50 shekels of silver)—in fact, he often had to pay a double dowry to make her a more desirable bride. The woman might decide to marry her attacker, or her father might decide the two should get married. In that case the attacker paid 50 shekels to her father and married the girl; and the law never allowed him to divorce her (Deut. 22:23-30). This protected the right of the woman.

The Bible outlawed kidnapping to stop the slave trade. This especially protected the foreigners (Exod. 22:21-24), the blind and deaf (Lev. 19:14, 33-34), the hired servants (Deut. 24:14), and other helpless people (Deut. 27:19).

If a woman attacked a man's genital organs, even to defend her husband, the law would cut off her hand (Deut. 25:11-12). This was the only case in which the Bible would allow the court to mutilate a guilty person. The Old Testament taught that God set man over woman, and every woman must respect this order of things.

If a man claimed that his wife had not been a virgin and her family could prove otherwise, the husband had to pay her father a massive fine—100 shekels of silver. He would be beaten, he would lose his right to divorce his wife, and he would have to support her for the rest of his life. In court, a judge would assume that the woman was innocent until proven guilty, and it took two witnesses to prove her guilt. If she was indeed guilty, she was put to death. But no man would dare to accuse his wife of adultery unless he was very sure of it, because a lie would bring bankruptcy and would make him his wife's servant forever (Deut. 22:13-19).

Another law that sheds light on the Bible's understanding of woman is found in Exodus 21:22-25. If two men were fighting and one of them struck a pregnant woman and she miscarried, the person who struck her was fined an amount determined by her husband, and administered by the judges. However, if the miscarriage caused further complicatons and she died, the law provided for the

Code of Lipit-Ishtar.
King of the small city kingdom of Isin in Sumer (nineteenth century B.C.), Lipit-Ishtar formulated a code of law to restore order to his kingdom. He probably derived most of his laws from existing Sumerian practices. The code contained 38 regulations dealing with matters such as the treatment of slaves, inheritance, and marriage.

death penalty. In this way unborn children and their mothers were valued and protected.

The law allowed no one to harm another person or his property. Notice the damages the offender had to pay in the matter of a goring ox (Exod. 21:28). God prized the rights of every person, and His Law protected them. A goring ox had to be locked up (Exod. 21:19), any open pit had to be covered (Exod. 21:33), and homeowners had to put railings around their roofs so that no one would fall off (Deut. 22:8).

5. Crimes against Property. God granted His people the right to own property, and He gave them special laws to protect that right. However, it is clear that the Bible placed a higher value on human life than on property. While murder carried the death penalty, theft carried only a fine. If someone stole an ox and couldn't return it, he had to pay its owner five times the normal value. If he stole a sheep, he had to pay four times the normal value. (Oxen were worth more because they were beasts of burden.) If the thief was able to return the beast he had stolen, he still had to pay the owner twice its value. If the thief couldn't afford to pay, he was sold into slavery to pay the debt (Exod. 22:1-5). And if the farmer discovered the thief at night and killed him, the judge would let the farmer go free.

God gave laws concerning "white-collar crime" too. If a person blackmailed a friend or refused to pay back a loan, a judge would order him to pay back what he had taken plus one-fifth more and to give a guilt offering to God (Lev. 6:1-7). If a merchant used false weights and measures, the courts would make him pay back the people he had cheated (Lev. 19:35-36; Deut. 25:13-16). The law required a person to return stray animals to their rightful owners; if he didn't know who the owner was, he was supposed to care for the animal until the owner claimed it (Exod. 23:4-5; Deut. 22:1-4).

A person who destroyed God's property received the full condemnation of the law. For example, God had ordered the leaders of Israel to place landmarks at the boundaries of each family's property. The Bible cursed anyone who moved these landmarks (Deut. 19:14; 27:17) because they belonged to God. The Bible also gave stern warnings to anyone who tampered with God's sanctuary (cf. Lev. 10:1-2).

H. Laws of Benevolence. Many biblical laws called for humane treatment of the poor and helpless, as well as kindness toward animals.

The law said that every animal was useful, and the Israelites were to feed each animal according to the work it did (Deut. 25:4). God did not allow his people to beat their animals cruelly. In fact, they had to let their animals rest on the Sabbath (Exod. 20:8-11; 23:72).

One law said that when an Israelite found a beast carrying a load that was too heavy for it—even if the animal belonged to his neighbor—he should take part of the burden himself (Deut. 22:1-4). The Israelites were supposed to leave gleanings in the field for wild animals to eat (Lev. 24: 4-7). Also, an Israelite could not take a mother bird and her eggs on the same day, nor a cow and its calf, nor a ewe sheep and its lamb (Lev. 22:28; Deut. 22:6-7). God's Law respected the source of life and demanded humane treament of all animals.

Scripture directed God's people to care for the widow, orphan, and foreigner (Exod. 22:22-24). These people did not receive handouts, however; they were supposed to be able to earn their own living (Deut. 24:19-22). The Israelites respected and cared for their elders (Lev. 19:32). They could criticize a neighbor they did not like, but they were not allowed to hold a grudge against him (Lev. 19:17-18). They could not inflict excessive punishment on a criminal (Deut. 25:1-3). In every way, God expected His people to love their neighbors.

If an Israelite loaned someone a coat or some other necessary item, it had to be returned at nightfall. An Israelite could not enter someone's house to collect a bad debt (Deut. 24:10-13). God honored the right of the creditor, but He also guarded the right of the debtor.

The law allowed travelers to enter a field and gather food to eat, but they could not carry off an extra supply (Deut. 23:24-25). A man had to pay wages to his hired hands every day, since they needed the money to buy their food (Deut. 24:14-15). He had to lend them money without interest in an emergency (Lev. 25:35-37). If a person could not make a living on his own, he could sign a contract to become another man's servant. His master had to treat him kindly, though (Lev. 25:39-43). A freeborn person could not be kidnapped and sold as a slave (Exod. 21:16; Deut. 24:7). And an Israelite had to protect a runaway slave from another country, making sure that his owner didn't harm him (Deut. 23:15-16). Each person could expect fair treatment under the legal system of Israel.

I. Personal and Family Rights. A survey of the laws of the Bible shows that they guard the rights of each individual and his family. The Law required children to respect and obey their parents and parents were supposed to raise their children to serve and obey God (Deut. 6:7). The Bible set strict limits on marriage to make sure that family life would be a decent and wholesome thing.

Each slave kept his dignity as a human being. No Israelite could be forced into slavery. Even if he signed a contract to become another man's servant, God's Law cancelled the contract at the end of 7 years (Exod. 21:2-6). A slave became a member of his owner's family. He enjoyed the rights of any other family member (except the right of inheritance, of course). If the slave was a foreigner, his owner could circumcise him and invite him to worship with other Jews (Exod. 12:44; Deut. 12:18; 16:10-11).

If an owner punished a slave so harshly that he died, the law branded him a murderer (Exod. 21:20). But if the slave did not die, the law did nothing; God judged that the owner suffered enough by having a disabled slave (Exod. 21:21). If the owner inflicted a permanent injury—for example, if the slave lost an eye or tooth—the slave could go free (Exod. 21:26-27).

Even though the Bible allowed slavery, its regulations reminded the Israelites that every person was created in the image of God—including the slave.

We've already noticed that the Bible preserved each person's right to his own property. He could claim any property that had been lost or stolen and anyone who borrowed his property had to return it in good condition. If the borrower lost the property or if it was stolen from him, he still had to repay the owner. In fact, if the borrower schemed to "lose" the property in his care, he had to repay the owner *twofold* (Exod. 22:7-15). When he borrowed another man's property, he held a sacred trust.

The Bible explained that God still owned all the land of the Israelites, even though it had been divided among the families of Israel (Lev. 25:23). Each seventh year the land was to enjoy a sabbath, during which no crops would be gathered; but any passer-by might take what he needed (Lev. 25:1-7). The ancient landmarks showed the boundary of each family's portion. If they rented or sold the land to someone else, the property came back to the family in the jubilee at the end of 50 years (Lev. 25:8-24). Even before the end of 50 years, the Law allowed a member of the family to buy the property back at its original price. If a man built a house inside a walled city, he could sell it. If he dd not buy it back within a year, it would not return to him in the jubilee (Lev. 25:29-31) But if a Levite sold his house, it would in any case be restored to him at that time (Lev. 25:32-34).

Because God owned the land, He dictated the rules of inheritance. God said that a firstborn son could receive a double portion of the property and other special benefits (Deut. 21:15-17; 25:6). A wicked son might receive nothing. And if there was no son, a daughter could inherit the property (Num 27:7-8). In that case, she had to marry a member of her own tribe to keep the property within the family (Num. 36:1-12). Anyone who inherited a piece of property had to use it to care for his relatives because he (or she) became the head of the family.

J. Obligations to God. The law of God did not simply describe the rights of each person; it also described his responsibilities to God. Each person owed his life to Yahweh, and so the community expected him to serve God and remain loyal to His people.

This is why biblical law contains so many religious commands. For example, God told His people to tear down heathen shrines and stop pagan worship practices (Deut. 7:5). He commanded them to observe the laws of the Sabbath and to regard His sanctuary with proper reverence (Lev. 19:30).

God bound His people to follow His law and no other. He commanded the leaders of Israel to record His law, and He commanded the people of Israel to study and remember it (Deut. 4:2; Num. 15:37-41; Lev. 18:4-5). God's Law demanded their reverence, obedience, and service. And as long as Israel obeyed God's commands, they lived in harmony with Him.

INTERTESTAMENTAL LAW

The Jewish notion of law changed somewhat between the writing of the Old and New Testaments. God had given His Word to the children of Israel through historic events—especially those involving Moses during the Exodus—and the later prophets and priests had interpreted that law for their own day. Their interpretation usually included a hope for national independence and superiority (Isa. 60:1-3; Jer. 31:3f.; Joel 3:18f.)—a hope that rested on the Jews' obedience to God's covenant. After centuries of failing to actualize this hope, the Jews saw this theme disappear from their prophecy. In fact, the role of prophecy itself diminished during the intertestamental period.

For the Jews, making the law meaningful for their own day became less important than making it meaningful for that future day when God would come to reward them. Thus they began to stress the law's ceremonial prescriptions. Almsgiving, festivals, ritual prayers, and temple rites grew to be very important in the Jewish community.

Disaster was looming on the horizon. The temple of Jersualem would be destroyed in A.D. 70 at the end of a bitter war between the Jews and the armies of Rome. This would affect the religious outlook of Jews and Christians alike—especially their hope for an immediate new age of the Messiah. The Jews would not be able to hold their festivals in the shambles of Jersualem, for the Roman army would completely end the possibility of temple worship. Early communities of Christians, realizing that Jesus' return was delayed, would develop a new organization. But the traditional

Jew would already have an organization to deal with the problems caused by the destruction of the temple. They would experience a shift in the balance of power between the religious parties, with the Pharisees emerging as the strongest Jewish faction.

The aristocratic Sadducees were closely connected with the temple, so their influence was to be destroyed when Jerusalem fell. The militant Zealots would lead the nation to the disastrous defeat, which would turn most Jews against them. The reclusive Essenes had always been a minority sect and would gain nothing from the war. But the Pharisees' concern for the law assumed them of a dominant place in Jewish life after the Roman conquest. They had developed many oral interpretations of the law for their own day, and after the fall of Jerusalem they would establish a new center for studying the law at Jamnia. There they would preserve and systematize the written law and their oral interpretations of it. This would be the beginning of modern Judaism, commonly called *rabbinic* Judaism.

The Jewish War came a generation after Jesus. But this preview of the war and its aftermath helps to set the stage for Jesus' dialogue with the Pharisees. The Gospels (especially Matthew) often picture Jesus in conflict with the Pharisees' interpretation of the law. This conflict foreshadowed the rift between the early Christians and Jews.

JESUS AND THE LAW

Jesus' attitude toward the law is a topic of much debate. Some scholars believe that He merely interpreted Mosaic Law like the Pharisees, without changing it. Others believe that Jesus penetrated past the letter of the law to reveal its great moral and spiritual principles. In more recent years, commentators have noted that some of Jesus' statements seem to be in direct conflict with the Mosaic Law. These commentators have made several attempts to resolve these conflicts. At least 3 of their interpretations have gained some popularity:

The first may be called *the fulfillment view*. Most readers are familiar with Jesus' statement, "Think not that I have come to abolish the law and the prophets; I have come not to abolish them but to fulfil them" (Matt. 5:17, RSV). There are apparent conflcts between Jesus' teachings and Mosaic Law (e.g., His teachings on divorce); but the fulfillment view tries to show that, if we look beyond appearances, we can harmonize Jesus' actions with the Old Testament in every case.

The second interpretation may be called *the sovereignty view*. Commentators who take this approach hold that, when there is a disagreeement between Jesus and Pharisaic law, Jesus' word is authoritative. They base this view upon Jesus' statements such as, " 'You have heard that it was said, "You shall love your neighbor, and hate your enemy." *But I say to you*' " (Matt. 5:43-44a, NASB, italics added). Exponents of the sovereignty view would point out that the Old Testament nowhere says, "You shall hate your enemy"; this was a teaching of the Pharisees.

The third interpretation might be called *the inscrutability view*. Commentators who favor this approach believe that we cannot determine Jesus' attitude toward the law. Even if we could determine His attitude, they doubt if it could be expressed in a clean, neat formula.

A. Dialogue with the Pharisees. But let us attempt to see what we can of the relationship between Jesus' teachings and Moses' Law, according to the biblical witness. We will rely heavily on the Gospel of Matthew, since Matthew and his audience were deeply concerned with Jewish matters.[2]

We find that Jesus said various things concerning the law. For example, in controversies such as that about eating on the Sabbath (Matt. 12:1-8), Jesus made it clear that He superseded the law. He said, "I tell you, something greater than the temple is here" (v. 6, RSV). The Pharisees were not looking for anything greater than the temple, where God's law was preserved. They were amazed to hear anyone claim that something was greater than the repository of God's Word. Christ not only refused to submit to their interpretation of the law, but He declared that He was greater than it: "Therefore the Son of man is Lord also of the sabbath" (Mark 2:28).

In other instances, though, Jesus preserved the law. For example, in Matthew 23:2ff., Jesus admonished the crowd to do all that the scribes and Pharisees told them, for they were the ones who upheld the traditions of the law of Moses. Then, however, He attacked the Pharisees' hypocrisy! Does this mean that Jesus changes

His position in the course of the sermon? Or is He making a distinction between the Pharisees' relaying Moses' Law faithfully and embroidering it falsely? Scholars disagree.

Second, Jesus emphasized that love is the proper motive for obeying God's Law. Pharisees would agree that love is important, but they had never said that everything else should be measured against it. The Pharisees had defined and redefined Mosaic Law so that it could be practiced as a complete code of righteousness. But for Jesus, righteousness did not depend upon following mechanically a prescribed pattern of action. His own love for other people often led Him to speak and act in ways that were unexpected and unconventional, as when He spoke harshly to the hostile Pharisees (Matt. 23:17; cf. Mark 3:5). This behavior did not fit any conventional idea of loving conduct; but Jesus' calculated

Marashu documents. A family of Jewish businessmen living in the Mesopotamian city of Nippur in the fifth century B.C. left behind a collection of over 700 tablets recording their commercial and real estate transactions. These clay documents include business contracts, land leases, loan contracts, and receipts. Nippur was a rich city, and some Jews who specialized in banking became quite wealthy there.

attempt to bring the Pharisees to their spiritual senses was the most loving gesture He could make to them.

Does Jesus bring a new and greater law? Or does He merely challenge the Pharisaic interpretations and hypocrisy? We see the dialogue between Jesus and the Pharisees in many circumstances, and more than one witness writes about it. But some common themes stand out:

—Jesus does not separate Himself from Mosiac Law (Matt. 5:17; Luke 9:31).

—Unlike the Pharisees, Jesus emphasizes God's love—though He does warn of God's judgment (Matt. 7:21).

—Jesus' behavior fits no mold of this world, He does not attempt to compete as a rabbi among rabbis, nor does He try to fill the traditional role of the Messiah. His relationship to the law is truly unique (cf. Matt. 7:28-29).

B. Jesus' Attitude. Jesus both affirms and criticizes the Jewish law. He does not teach that fulfillment of the Mosaic Law means that one automatically enters into the saving relationship between God and His people that He calls God's "Kingdom." Rather, He says that people enter that Kingdom through faith in Christ Himself, and that it produces a completely regenerated life. Jesus teaches that we should obey God because He is our heavenly Father and we love Him; we do not obey in order to be made right wih Him.

PAUL AND THE LAW

Paul affirms and criticizes the law. He declares that God is finished with it, but also that He has established it. Many of Paul's teachings on this subject are very strongly stated: "For Christ is the end of the law for righteousness to every one that believeth" (Rom. 10:4). "Do we then make void the law through faith? God forbid: yea, we establish the law" (Rom 3:31). "For I through the law am dead to the law, that I might live unto God" (Gal. 2:19).

How may we integrate these divergent emphases?

A. Paul's World. To make sense of this tension in Paul's teachings, we need to understand the times in which he lived. When Paul wrote, Jerusalem was still intact. The Sadducees and Zealots were powers to be reckoned with, but there was no unified Jewish opposition to Christianity. Paul was part of a fledgling religious community that took its place alongside the other Jewish sects.

When the church began to spread into Gentile territory, a serious question arose: Should Gentiles who are unfamiliar with the law be required to learn and practice it when they become Christians?

B. The Jerusalem Council. Acts 15 and Galations 2 (by common interpretation) tell how the church convened an apostolic council to decide this issue. The congregation at Jerusalem was headed by James, brother of Jesus and the successor of Peter, whose leadership had been ended by Herod Agrippa (Acts 12:17; 15:13; 21:18; Gal. 1:19). James believed that the Jewish Christians should obey Jewish law, but that Gentile Christians could be permitted a certain amount of freedom from it. A dissenting faction existed, though (Acts 15:5; Gal. 2:4). The dissenters believed that all Christians should obey the Jewish law; they are therefore called the "Judaizers."

The real conflict came between James' faction and Paul's followers, who may have been more liberal than James (note Gal. 2–4f.). Paul was summoned to Jerusalem to validate his preaching (Gal. 2:1-3), particularly on the relation of the Law to the gospel of Christ. The outcome was a brotherly agreement between Paul, James, and Peter. In principle, they agreed that the Gentile congregations were free from most of the Law, and they recognized that faith in Christ was sufficient to save the Gentiles.

This principle confirmed Jesus' teaching that law is not to be obeyed as a fetish, or as a system of salvation, since faith in Christ saves people. This principle came to dominate the early church, and it served as a springboard for Paul's rather sophisticated theology of law and gospel.

Unlike Jesus, who wrote nothing that we know of, Paul wrote weighty doctrinal and pastoral letters. Although some of them circulated among serveral churches (cf. Col. 4:16), Paul often wrote with the local problems of a particular congregation in his mind.

For this reason, he seems to have different opinions on the law in different letters. At Corinth, for example, Paul's opponents were Hellenistic; they had little use for law or morality. Paul took a very conservative stand in responding to them. In Galatia, on the other hand, he had to face the Judaizers. So Paul emphasized liberty from law when writing this letter.

After Paul left the Jerusalem Council, he ministered primarily to Hellenistic Jewish communities. Their people had some notion of Jewish law mixed with Gentile ideas. In most congregations, Jewish Christians worshiped beside Gentile Christians. One group was expected to obey the law; the other was released from most of it. It is no wonder that the issue of law required so much of Paul's attention.

C. Paul's Theme of Faith vs. Law. Probably the most dominant theme in all of Paul's writings is that the Law is subordinate to faith in Christ: "A man is not justified by works of the law but through faith in Jesus Christ" (Gal. 2:16; cf. Phil. 3; Rom. 1–4). Paul taught that no law brings justification in and of itself. The new covenant is based on the work of the Holy Spirit in the heart, and not on "letters in stone" (an obvious reference to Mosaic Law). Paul knew that God's law can be made the basis of a legalistic, self-justifying habit of mind; and when it is thus abused we are doomed "under law." This legal condemnation is the opposite of being "under grace"—the grace, that is, of Christ's redeeming death (Rom. 6:14). Paul does not attack the righteous content of the Law, but the lethal manner in which it operates.

In what way has the law been superseded by faith in Christ? Paul declares that all of us, Jews and Gentiles, have been under the judgment of the Law (Rom. 5:12-19), but Christ freed us from this judgment through the cross (Gal. 2:21; Rom. 7:4; 8:1ff.). All of Paul's preaching centers on Christ crucified (1 Cor. 1:17ff.). If we are to understand his attitude toward the law, we must therefore see it in light of Jesus' Crucifixion.

Paul understood that Jesus died to open for us a way of salvation (Gal 2:21). That is, Christ died so that we might cease from trying to right ourselves with God by obeying the law. Jesus substituted Himself for us, taking our judgment upon Himself so that we would not have to bear it (2 Cor. 5:19-21; Gal. 3:13; Col. 2:14).

7

WARFARE AND WEAPONS

Early in the Book of Genesis we find warfare going on (the battle of the kings, chap. 14). The human pattern of war continues right to the end of the Book of Revelation, where the final battle between good and evil (Armageddon) is foretold.

As we survey the biblical material on warfare, we find that it falls into two categories: what the Bible says about war (teaching) and what actually happened (history).

HOW THE OLD TESTAMENT DEALS WITH WAR

We can make some basic observations about the Old Testament's ideas of war and teachings concerning it. These ideas changed slightly in New Testament times.

A. Promotion of Justice. Properly conducted warfare was tied to defending and promoting justice and righteousness. Theologian John Murray builds a strong case for the just waging of war by comparing it to the power God gave to the civil magistrate (cf. Rom. 13:1-7; 1 Pet. 2:13-17).[1] This general principle was applied to national security, and Israel was organized into a fighting unit (Exod. 7:4; 12:51) to be led by God Himself into battle (Judg. 4:14; cf. Deut. 20:4). Whenever wars were fought under God's leadership, they were considered "holy" wars; they were for the purpose of establishing Israel in the Promised Land or protecting them from foreign invasions. In these "holy" wars, going into battle was preceded by sacrificing to God (1 Sam. 7:9; 13:9, 12) and consulting Him as the Leader of Israel's armies (Judg. 20:22, 28; 1 Sam. 14:37; 23:2, 4). So in the Old Testament God used war for just and righteous ends to promote and protect righteousness.

B. God's Protection. In a properly conducted "holy" war God promised His protection of the warriors (Deut. 20:1-4). Israel's

Weapons from Palestine. These relics of war date from between the ninth and the early sixth centuries B.C. They include arrowheads, spearheads, daggers, and a sword.

enemies were God's enemies, and the people were called on to trust Him, rather than their own strength, for victory (Judg. 5:31; see Exod. 17:16). When they did this, God fought on their side, kept them from bodily harm, and sometimes used the forces of nature against the enemy (cf. Josh. 10:11; 24:7; and many other passages).

C. God's Presence. The ark of the covenant served as a symbol or sign of God's presence with the Israelites during battle (Exod. 30:6; cf. 25:21-22). During the wanderings in the wilderness and in the conquest of the Promised Land the ark always went before the armies of Israel. This was to *symbolize* God's active presence with His people, not to suggest that His presence was localized in that object (1 Kings 8:21), or that the bringing of the ark was like a magic spell. At one time, however, the people made the mistake of thinking that the ark as a physical object assured them of God's presence and guaranteed them victory (1 Sam. 4:1-11). David, on the other hand, took the ark into battle too (2 Sam. 11:11); but it appears that his trust was in God to win the battle, not in the ark as an object. His understanding of God's guidance was like that of Israel during the conquest of the Promised Land.

D. Ritual Cleanness. If God was to fight with and for His people, they were to be ritually clean (Deut. 23:9-14). Because they were to be completely separate from anything having to do with sin and pollution, God gave them strict instructions on what they were to do, and the people in turn made strong vows to the Lord (1 Sam. 21:4-5; 2 Sam. 11:11; cf. Exod. 19:15). The people and their cause were to be holy, for God would fight only in a war that was holy and just.

E. Victory Expected. The priests were to blow trumpets before battle to place their cause before God, to show that they expected victory, and to give God thanks for it (Num. 10:9-10). In the course of particular battles, trumpets often served as the means of sending instructions from the commanders to their troops (Josh. 6:5; Judg. 3:27; 7:16-17). The armies of Israel also plunged into battle using a war cry, sometimes consisting of a loud yell and sometimes a loud petition to God. A similar cry was used in the worship of the Lord (Lev. 23:24; Num 29:1).

F. Military Conscription. In Israel's earlier history the army consisted of all men who were 20 years or older (Num. 1:2-3, 18, 20, 45; 26:2-4). Some scholars have suggested that 50 was the upper limit for soldiers, just as it was for the priests (cf. Num. 4:3, 23). At other times there seems to have been a selective service system for particular battles in which only a limited number of men fought (Num. 31:3-6).

G. Other Priorities. Certain social responsibilities had priority over warfare, and several categories of eligible men were exempted from a particular battle or war.

First, anyone who had recently built a home and had not dedicated it was excused (Deut. 20:5). Second, anyone who had planted a vineyard and not yet harvested it was not required to go to war (Deut. 20:6). Third, anyone who had just married and not yet consummated his marriage could stay at home (Deut. 20:7). In fact, the newly married were to be exempted for a year (Deut. 24:5). Fourth, any who were afraid or disheartened were to be excused, for they could demoralize the troops (Deut. 20:8). Fifth, Levites did not have to go to war (Num. 1:48-49), though a number of them voluntarily took up arms. Family and religious obligations had priority over going to war.

H. Peace Offered. Before distant cities were to be attacked, peace terms were to be offered them (Deut. 20:10-15). The terms of this peace included the subjection of the enemy to slavery or forced labor, which in effect made them vassals of Israel. Historical records from this period show that often these peace treaties were framed in a particular form, in which the vassal pledged his total obedience to the overlord while the latter promised protection to his vassal. To break this treaty was to rebel against the overlord and forfeit his mercy, protection, and any other blessings.

1. Utter Destruction. War was a grim and ugly affair. The instructions for the conquest of the Promised Land were that all the inhabitants that were found alive were to be destroyed lest they lead the people of God into their awful perversions (Deut. 20:16-18). Everything within Palestine proper was to be consecrated to God, and no treaty or covenant was to be made with these peoples (Deut. 2:34; 3:6; Josh. 11:14; and many other passages).

It is important to note that the ban on taking any kind of spoil in Canaan was more than a wartime regulation. It was part of the regular worship of God and included anything that was totally consecrated to Him (Num. 18:14; Lev. 27:21, 28-29). Since Palestine was the land God had claimed for Himself, He demanded that the entire land be consecrated to Him. In practice this meant that the land had to be thoroughly purified, for no unholy person or thing could stand in His presence and He was going to dwell in this land with His people. The Canaanites, who had been cursed in their distant ancestor (Gen. 9:25), had given themselves to dreadful sinfulness and practiced awful perversions of virtually every form as religious acts.

We should also note that every man is already under the sentence of death by God, and lives only by His grace (Gen. 3:3), so there needs to be no further justification of God's curse on any man, including the Canaanites. Their abominations, however, went even beyond those of other sinful men. Furthermore, as the eternal Creator and sovereign Lord of the universe, God controls the lifespan of every person (Psa. 31:15; 39:4-5; Job 1:21; cf. Dan. 4:35). So whether death comes by natural means or through war, it is strictly in His hands.

Nations outside Palestine that refused Israel's offer of peace and bondage received death for every man; all the women, children, livestock, and everything else became booty for the Israelites (Deut. 20:12-14). Exceptions to these rules came either through specific divine directions (Num. 31:7; 2 Sam. 8:2) or through Israel's own disobedience (e.g., 1 Sam. 30:17). Women prisoners could be taken as wives and thus made to serve the Lord. In this case, they would not later be subjected to slavery, which was to be their lot otherwise (Deut. 21:10-14).

J. Trust in God. The people of Israel were to trust in God and not in their own military strength. God originally planned for His people's government to be centralized in Him rather than in a human king, and that would have meant a minimum of taxation. Strong earthly rulers tend to require heavy taxation. Since cavalry and chariots as major military weapons of the time were extremely expensive to acquire and maintain, God forbade Israelite kings to have them (Deut. 17:16). They would have required a highly centralized government and very high taxes.

K. Respect for Natural Resources. God forbade the destruction of fruit trees to build siege machinery in attacking walled cities (Deut. 20:19-20). Even in times of warfare Israel was taught to respect the fruit of the ground, which was a source of life, and was reminded that war was against sinful men and not against nature.

L. Compensation for Troops. Adequate provision was made for paying the troops (Num. 31:21-31, 42; Deut. 20:14), binding their families to outfit and support them, and allowing them to take booty as their pay (1 Sam. 30:16; Psa. 119:162; Isa. 9:3). The booty was to be divided among all the troops, including those who were "behind the lines" caring for the baggage or waiting at the

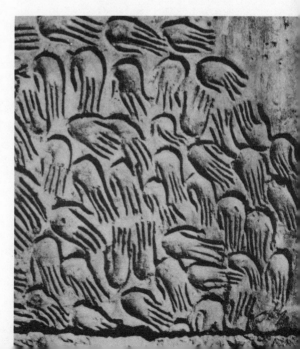

Heap of hands. This limestone relief shows hands that were severed by the soldiers of Rameses III in their victory over the Libyans (*ca.* 1190 B.C.). This was common practice among the Egyptians, who used the hands to tally the number of enemy dead.

rear for some other reason (Num. 31:26-47; Judg. 5:30; 1 Sam. 30:24-25).

A portion also had to be set aside for the Lord (Num. 31:28-30, 50-54; Josh. 6:24). In later Israelite history the king, as God's special representative, took the Lord's portion for the temple (2 Sam. 8:7-8, 11) and for the palace or the maintenance of government (2 Sam. 12:30; cf. 1 Sam. 21:9; 2 Kings 14:14).

These are 12 general observations on the rules or principles of warfare in the Old Testament. The biblical record of the history of Israel shows repeated violations of them. Almost from the beginning of their history in the land, idolatry and superstition led the people away from the Lord. We see this in the idolatrous behavior of the judges Gideon and Micah (Judg. 8:22-28; 17:1-6). Later, the monarchy under Saul was founded on the same lack of trust in God. Solomon's large standing army and many chariots bear clear evidence of his attitude toward God's earlier instructions. Finally, during the divided monarchy, the kings of Israel and Judah paid little attention to the directives of God concerning warfare.

Interestingly, even though modern secular man often harshly condemns what he thinks to be the barbarity of biblical war regulations, today's wars are conducted on a much more barbaric level, sparing neither land nor people. And this is just as true in wars between nations as it is in civil wars where various factions strive for the control of a particular country. We have developed weapons so destructive that they know no distincton between the military and civilians. The morality of warfare and those who fight in wars is lost in today's world because men basically disregard the issues of righteousness and justice. On the battlefield the end justifies the means, hate predominates, and no rules prevail.

NEW TESTAMENT TEACHINGS

In the New Testament the emphasis is again on righteousness and justice. The issues are too complicated to discuss in detail; but Scripture suggests a Christian position on war.

It is clear that many practices of modern warfare must be denounced strongly. On the other hand, the same God is at the center of both Testaments; and in the Old Testament, God engaged in war Himself (Exod. 7:4; 12:41; 14:14; 15:1). He used war to punish His people (Deut. 28:49-57) and to judge the nations (1 Sam. 15:1-3).

A. The Principle of Love. We see that love undergirds both the Law of Moses and the teachings of Jesus. Both command the pious person to love God totally (Deut. 6:5 and Matt. 22:37) and his neighbor as himself (cf. Lev. 19:18 and Matt. 22:39). Warfare for the cause of justice and righteousness—that is, waging war in defense of God or one's neighbor—is therefore an expression of love and is not contrary to the ethic of Jesus.

B. Sinful Man. According to the New Testament, man is still the same—a sinner who pursues evil ways (cf. James 4:1-4). John Murray has written, "War arises from failure to conform to the attitudes and principles inculcated by the Lord. If there were no sin there would be no war."[2] But sin is, in fact, universal.

Yet the world cries out for justice, and the Christian's ear should be open to this cry. "Love is not inconsistent with the infliction of punishment for wrong. Love is first of all love to God, and therefore love of justice."[3] The New Testament writers maintain that God has brought government into being for the purpose of maintaining justice, and for those in power to be able to do that, He has given them the power and authority to wage war. Governments are to use this power—not vindictively, maliciously, or hatefully against other men—but as a means of protection and the carrying out of justice. It is interesting to note that many biblical passages that deal with the last times are full of references to warfare conducted by God or under His orders (cf. Matt. 24:6; Isa. 2:4; and many others).

C. Unanswered Questions. The New Testament leaves many important questions unanswered. Thus, if governments have the right to wage warfare for a just cause, who determines whether a cause is just? Is it up to the individual Christian? Does this mean that every Christian (or a group of Christians) must have access to all information the government has with regard to the declaration of war? If this access is not given, may he (or they) refuse to participate?

Again, if a nation is justified in protecting its territory, what constitutes a nation and who determines what its territorial limits are? (Was the settling of America an act of aggression against a na-

Egyptian soldiers. These models of Nubian and Egyptian soldiers march in 4 columns of 10 each. The darker skinned Nubians carry bows and arrows while the Egyptians are armed with lances and shields. These models, found in an Egyptian tomb, date from about 2000 B.C.

tion? If so, should the United States government return the whole territory to its original owners? Who can determine how this territory might be subdivided among them?)

Once more, how should a Christian conduct himself in the midst of war and battle? Should he give, for instance, aid to wounded enemies?

These questions need careful study, for the Bible does not give cut-and-dried answers to them.

THE CONDUCT OF WAR

Let us examine the historical record of war in the Old Testament and the weapons used throughout the four historical periods of Israel's existence.

A. The Period of the Patriarchs. This period was characterized by mass movements and wanderings of many peoples in the Near East. These movements brought different peoples into contact with one another, both peacefully and through warfare. They were quick to learn from these contacts, and the knowledge of the art of warfare grew accordingly.

During this period the light chariot first appeared, and its use spread from Asia Minor to Egypt. This period also saw the invention and use of the battering ram, metal breastplates, and metal helmets, and the development of countermeasures against them. The response to the battering ram was the "casemated" wall (a term used for walls thickened with a space, sometimes a room, between the outer wall itself and the inner layer of stone). The composite bow or crossbow was used against the light chariot. These new weapons, including the piercing axe, helmets, and shields, greatly changed warfare during that time. They also enabled armies who used them (like the Hyksos) to conquer those who did not have them (like the Egyptians).

The Hebrew patriarchs fought only in the first half of this period (*ca.* 2166–1805 B.C.). The weapons used at this time differed somewhat between the Egyptians to the south of Palestine and the nations north of Palestine. Abraham and his allies probably used the latter kind.

Egyptian warriors of this period were protected by shields and wore no armor, as did their neighbors to the north. The axe in Egypt was designed primarily to be used against soldiers without armor, while other peoples used axes designed to penetrate armor. Semites introduced the eye-axe, or penetrating axe, into Egypt. But it was not generally accepted there. Some Semitic warriors carried a refined eye-axe (also called a duck-bill axe), with a handle that was often curved to increase leverage.

The sword of this period first appeared several centuries before and is called a sickle sword. It became prominent during the period of the Israelite conquest of Canaan. This was a curved cutting sword that was made from a single piece of metal and easily wielded in battle, even from a chariot. Soldiers also fought with many varieties of short straight swords or daggers, which were designed primarily for hand-to-hand combat.

Spears and javelins of this early period were attached to wooden stocks by a tang; the base was sometimes tipped with metal so the weapon could be stuck into the ground when not in use. The blunt edge could also be used as a club. These weapons were standard equipment in armies from this time on. Archaeological evidence associates these javelins, spears, and short narrow daggers with the nomadic Semites who invaded Palestine from the north.

Long-range weapons of this period consisted of the bow and the sling. Soldiers mainly used the simple double-convex bow, while other types of simple bows are found in Egyptian tomb paintings and actually buried in the tombs. When not in use, bows are unstrung. The quiver for the arrows was a Semitic invention used rarely by the Egyptians, who preferred to carry their arrows in bundles which they piled at their feet while shooting. The bow was used as both an offensive and a defensive weapon in all kinds of battles. Slingmen were used especially in siege warfare in support of archers.

This period also shows the existence of fortresses, such as Buhen in Egypt, which is similar to Palestinian fortifications of this period. Egypt also began using battering rams during this period.

The only battle in the Bible during this period fought by the Hebrew patriarchs was the surprise attack of Abraham on the four kings of the north (Gen. 14). We have no details of the battle tactics—apart from the surprise—or the weapons used, but the previous discussion gives us some idea of what Abraham and his soldiers might have used.

Archaeological evidence shows the development of new and improved weapons in the last half of the patriarchal period. Narrow-socketed axes have now been designed for even greater armor penetration, and socketed spears and javelins now begin to appear, since the tang attachment often caused the staff to split. In the 1500s B.C. the composite bow, one that had greater range and penetration, made its appearance in Palestine. It was expensive to make and more easily affected by weather conditions, so it was not only unstrung when not in use but carried in a case. It must have been during this period that the heavier chariot became a major weapon, for there is little evidence that the Egyptians and Semites used it earlier as such.

B. The Period of the Egyptian Captivity through the Period of the Judges. This period was very important in the Near East, for it saw the rise of many warlike peoples, further migrations, and much conflict. Egypt was on the rise again; the Hittites emerged as a mighty military power; the Hebrews—now called Israelites—invaded Palestine; and the Sea People appeared on the coast of Palestine, introducing new weapons to the Near East. These included the long straight sword, smaller face shields, and better armor, including coats of mail or scaled armor. The composite bow became a major weapon in the hands of the major powers.

Because of the rise of new powers, weapons in this period went through considerable changes. The cutting sickle sword was improved by making the blade longer in comparison to the hilt. This one-edged sword perhaps explains the phrase "smite with the edge of the sword" (in Joshua and Judges), in which the victim was killed by the one edge of the sickle sword. The straight sword or dagger was refined because of the improvement in armor, which made the sickle sword obsolete. In addition to the dagger, a long straight sword made its appearance toward the end of the period, being brought into the Near East by the Sea People, among whom were the Philistines. It was originally Aegean in design.

The spear and the axe continued to be the basic weapons of the infantry. We find that Barak's forty thousand troops in Israel had neither sword nor spear (Judg. 5:8), and toward the end of the per-

Sickle sword. The sickle sword was commonly used during the time of the Israelite conquest of Canaan. A curved cutting sword made of a single piece of metal, the weapon was easily wielded in battle. Its cutting edge was the outer edge of the bow, unlike the sickles used in agriculture.

Coat of mail. This fragment of a Hurrian coat of mail (made of bronze plates laced together with cord or thongs) was probably from an unfinished piece of armor. Discovered at Nuzi in Iraq, the armor dates from about 1400 B.C. The Hurrians lived in northern Mesopotamia; some scholars identify them as the Horites (cf. Gen. 36:20-29).

iod the Philistines totally disarmed the Israelites (cf. 1 Sam. 13:19-22).

The chariots of the Assyrians, Canaanites, and Hittites had three riders—a driver, a man who carried the shield as defense, and the bowman or spearman. The spear was also the weapon of the driver and was carried in a special holder at the back of the chariot.

The difficult-to-make composite bow came into fuller use at this time, in both its triangular and its recurved form. Arrows were usually made of reeds, and battle arrowheads were made of bronze and were spined to help them penetrate armor. Quivers holding 25 to 30 arrows came into general use in this period. (Quite a comment on Psa. 127:5 in terms of the number of children!)

Various types of shields were used during this period: the rectangular, slightly convex shield, the rectangular with a rounded top shield (Egyptian), the light round shield (introduced by and at first used exclusively by the Sea People), and the "figure eight" shield of the Hittites.

Armor became much more widely used by the major military powers especially in conjunction with archery and chariot units. The disadvantages of armor were its excessive weight, which curtailed the ability of soldiers to move well, and the expense and difficulty of its manufacture. Soldiers also began to be equipped with helmets (another expensive piece of military equipment introduced by the Semites). The piercing axe was then improved further to combat the effectiveness of the helmet and armor.

Chariots became increasingly important weapons for the Egyptians, whose words for the horses and chariots were Canaanite because of their origin. This equipment also was expensive to build and maintain, but was highly effective in battle.

Fortifications were used extensively in Palestine, as material for building strong and thick walls was readily available. Aramaean fortifications of this period seem to have been *casemated*. This kind of wall was strengthened regularly by supporting balconies and crenellated parapets or battlements. Yigael Yadin has described crenellated parapets as looking like a row of teeth with gaps between them. The "teeth" are called *merlons*, while the "gaps" are called *embrasures* or *crenels*. All this provided the defenders with ex-

Catapults

For about 2,000 years, catapults and other "engines of war" were feared as horrible weapons of destruction and death. As early as the eighth century B.C., the Bible mentions that Uzziah "made in Jerusalem engines, invented by cunning men, to be on the towers and upon the bulwarks, to shoot arrows and great stones withal" (2 Chron. 26:15). The *catapult* was any type of war machine that could throw stones or arrows.

The simplest catapult (sometimes called *ballista*) was designed like a giant crossbow on a carriage. A more complex type had a rectangular wooden frame that housed a mechanical arm to hurl stones or arrows. Twisted rope, mule gut, or other animal sinew was wound around levers to create tension which, when released, propelled these objects through the air.

Some catapults could be carried in pieces by man or mule and assembled quickly on the battlefield. Alexander the Great was fond of these portable models. But most catapults were larger, sacrificing mobility for additional weight and force. The average range of a catapult was between 315 and 450 m. (350 and 500 yds.). It could throw a 2.5 m. (8 ft.) javelin or a 13 kg. (30 lb.) stone.

During the siege of a city, a cata-pult could be kept out of the enemy archers' range. But large catapults were a disadvantage on the open battlefield, since they could not be easily moved if the enemy gained ground. A large catapult was helpless when it lost its advantage of range.

Some large catapults became almost legendary. The Roman catapult used at the siege of Carthage in 149–146 B.C. weighed several tons and threw to a distance of 360 m. (400 yds.). There are accounts of catapults with ranges up to 720 m. (860 yds.), but their accuracy was quite limited.

The inhabitants of a besieged city could never be sure what a catapult might hurl over their walls. While stones and arrows were the usual ammunition, flaming mixtures of sulphur and oil were sometimes used to set fire to the city. A catapult could also throw decaying animals or dead bodies into a city to cause disease among its population. Perhaps this was the earliest form of germ warfare.

Catapults and ballistas became obsolete with the development of more accurate and maneuverable cannons. But from 800 B.C. to A.D. 1500, they served as the most formidable weapons on the world scene.

cellent protection and effective angles to shoot at the enemy. The distance between the towers and battlements was never more than double the range of the defending archers. Smaller fortresses were called *migdolim,* the Hebrew term for "towers" (cf. Judg. 9:50-52; 2 Chron. 26:10; 27:4).

Battering rams were used to attack fortresses, but the Canaanites thickened the walls of their cities so that they were ineffective. Defenders would often begin their stand outside the wall, where they had greater mobility. They would then fall back into the city or be drawn up the walls by ropes if they were unsuccessful (cf. Josh. 2:15). From the tops of the walls the defenders would shoot arrows, throw spears and javelins, and drop stones and anything else that was movable on the attackers who might be climbing up scaling ladders, seeking to undermine the walls, attacking the walls and gates with battering rams, or trying to burn or hack through the city gates. The siege was complicated and costly in human life and money, so usually the attacking commander tried various means to capture the city without a siege. The attacking army would often build barriers, temporary walls, and bulwarks around its camp (cf. Deut. 20:19-20) to prevent sneak attacks by the defenders or from any allies that might come to their aid.

All these descriptions suggest that the Israelites faced tremendous opposition when they were on the threshold of entering the Promised Land (note the fortified cites of Deut. 1:28 and 3:5 and the iron chariots of Josh. 17:16-18). These former slaves were probably armed with Egyptian hand weapons (Exod. 11:2) and any other arms captured from enemies during the 40 years of wandering. Moses, who had been trained in all the necessary arts in Egypt, including warfare, must have trained the people accordingly. This does not mean that they had become a well-trained, professional army, for Israel had been taught to depend totally on God. He was to be the One who brought them victory and intervened when they obeyed Him. The biblical account records many battles during their wilderness years (cf. Exod. 17:8-16; Num. 21:3, 23-25, 32, 35), but we are not given any details except that they were won or lost according to God's intervention. The key to their victories was their dependence on the intervention of God.

We also know that every man except those exempted served in the army, which was organized according to units of 1,000, 100,

50, and 10 (cf. Num. 2). Every man in the army supplied his own weapons (see Num. 31:3; 32:20), applied or did not apply the ban according to God's directions (see Num. 11:2-11, 16-20), and divided the booty among all the people and the Lord. The army was mustered by various means, including the setting up of poles on hills, fire signals, ad trumpets. Communication in battle was maintained by messengers on foot (Judg. 9:31; cf. 2 Sam. 11:19; 18:19) or on horseback (2 Kings 9:17-18), by fire signals (Judg. 20:38; cf. Jer. 6:1), and by trumpets (Jer. 6:1).

The account of the conquest of the Promised Land tells us something of the battle tactics Israel used. They used a trick to draw the defenders of Ai out of their strongly fortified city (Josh. 8:3-22; cf. Judg. 20:29-41) and later confronted the chariots of the Canaanites and defeated them (Josh. 17:18). The overall strategy they used was to "divide and conquer." They invaded central Palestine, then turned south, and finally smashed the opposition in the north after a forced march by night. After the conquest they occupied the mountain regions, while the previous inhabitants still lived on the plains and coastal areas.

During the period of the judges each tribe pretty much went its own way and suffered for it, as various groups of peoples invaded the land. Some military cooperation did exist among the tribes (cf. Judg. 7:24), and once involved them all (Judg. 21:8-9). Most of their suffering and captivity came as a result of their disobeying the Mosaic Covenant of Sinai, with the result that God brought on them the punishments He had promised.

New tactics developed during this period as the tribes began to learn the art of warfare. Ehud assassinated Eglon with a short double-edged sword or dagger, which he had bound to his right side and smuggled past the bodyguards (Judg. 3:21). Barak lured the chariots of Sisera into the muddy flats of the Kishon River and destroyed him and his army (Judg. 5:21). Gideon used the unexpected tactic of a small raiding force that made much noise and surprised the Midianites at night with the added effect of lights in the hills (Judg. 7:16-22). Then, after the enemy was routed, Gideon summoned his reserve troops to the pursuit (vv. 23-25).

On one occasion the men of Succoth asked Gideon if he had the hands of two Midianite kings in his possession; they would not give his army food unless he had them (Judg. 8:6). This was a practice of the Egyptians and Assyrians, who amputated the hands of their enemies as proof of their victories and enemy casualties.

We are given many details of Abimelech's capture of the tower or fortress of Shechem (cf. Judg. 9). The battle had two stages. In

Gold dagger and sheath. The hilt of this beautifully made weapon from Ur (*ca.* twenty-fifth century B.C.). is a single piece of lapis lazuli, studded with gold and pierced by a hole edged with gold. The mark on the golden blade may identify the owner. The gold sheath is decorated with an openwork design of woven grass.

the first, the open battle before the city, Abimelech divided his troops into three units and attacked at dawn—common tactics of the day. In the second stage he attacked the fortress, breached the walls, and burned down the inner citadel.

Toward the end of this period we find that the tribe of Benjamin had trained 700 slingers, who were lefthanded and never missed (Judg. 20:16). We also discover that the recruited army of the other tribes numbered some 400,000 men, a large force indeed by any standards (Judg. 20:17). However, the large numbers quoted in the Old Testament have been questioned for centuries.

During the second half of this period we find the Egyptians and the Canaanites engaged in many battles. Egyptian tomb paintings show the chariots of the battling armies and the warfare against the Sea People. The Canaanites used three-man chariots, while the Egyptians used two men to man their chariots. Infantrymen carried two spears, a long straight sword, and a round shield; they fought in groups of four and marched in unison into battle. The Egyptians used mercenaries (often other Sea People) as their first striking force and as bodyguards in the palace to guard the pharaoh against any local intrigues.

Finally, we have one fascinating detail of how a city was breached in the account of the capture of Bethel. The Israelites spotted a man coming out of the city and forced him to tell them of the secret tunnel into the city. They came through it, surprised the inhabitants, and killed everyone in it except the man who had shown them the way in (Judg. 1:22-26). These secret entryways were used for launching attacks on the besiegers or as ways of escape should the city fall. The Israelites simply reversed the process.

C. The Period of the United Monarchy. In the early part of this period the Hittite kingdom all but vanished from the pages of history and the Egyptians were in decline. This helped the rise of a strong Israelite kingdom under Saul, David, and Solomon. Militarily the strength of Israel would not be broken till after the death of Solomon, when the Pharaoh Shishak took and looted Jerusalem during the reign of Rehoboam (*ca.* 925 B.C.; cf. 1 Kings 14:25-26).

During Saul's rule wars were fought pretty much as before. With the rise of the kingdom came the need for training, and the Bible mentions Saul's son Jonathan as an instructor in the use of the bow (2 Sam. 1:18); some scholars believe this passage to be a reference to instruction in warfare. This period saw the use of the bronze bow, which was probably a compound bow covered with bronze (cf. 2 Sam. 22:35; Psa. 18:34). One type of shield used by the Israelites was large and went with a man armed with a spear, while another was used with the bow to protect the archer.

Tactically the army was divided into three units and used the surprise attack of late night and early morning (cf. Judg. 7:16; 9:43; 1 Sam. 11:11; 14:36). With a king on the throne, a standing army was organized (apparently also into three units; 1 Sam. 13:2), fulfilling the request of the people for a king and an army. The Philistines against whom Saul fought had infantry (also organized into three units; 1 Sam. 13:17), chariots, and cavalry.

One of the interesting devices used by opposing Near Eastern armies was the tactic of the duel. Each army selected a champion, they fought one another, and the one who won represented victory for his army. The outcome of the duel determined the outcome of the war, and no additional battles were fought. So Goliath, the Philistine champion (who was perhaps 9½ feet tall), challenged Israel to send out a man to fight him. The meaning of the Hebrew term translated "champion" (KJV) has the connotation of "dueler"; Goliath may have been a professional dueler (1 Sam. 17:4-10). His weapons consisted of the long sword in a scabbard (1 Sam. 17:51), a bronze helmet, armor on his body and legs, and a spear (1 Sam. 17:5-7). His large shield was carried by his shield-bearer, a common practice of the time.

The potential duel was an ideal solution for Saul's army if they could but find someone to fight the giant Philistine. It would prevent many casualties for his outmanned force. When David finally volunteered for the duel, the Philistine made fun of him. The only weapon David had was a sling, and the Sea People did not use such a weapon, so Goliath saw no threat in it. Since he did not carry a bow, David's sling considerably outdistanced Goliath's close-combat weapons. And the tactical advantage—not to mention the help of the Lord—was with him.

A mass duel was fought later between David and the descendants of Saul. But because the duelists all killed one another, the armies subsequently fought and David was victorious (cf. 2 Sam. 2:12-17). Tomb pictures from Tel Halaf of the same period show duelists in action. There may have been certain rules for dueling, for we see the combatants grabbing one another by the hair and trying to finish each other off with daggers (cf. 2 Sam. 2:16).

Two additional sidelights on warfare of the time come in David's capture of Jerusalem for his capital (2 Sam. 5:6-8). After carefully studying the "tunnel" of Jerusalem ("gutter" in the KJV, v. 8), some archaeologists have concluded that it was too narrow for a man to get through.[4] They suggest that the Hebrew word, used only here and in Psalm 42:7, might be rendered *trident,* a three-pronged sea weapon. Thus the New English Bible translates the phrase: "Let him use his grapplingiron," probably also a three-

War Galleys

The mainstay of navies in the ancient Mediterranean world was the war galley. This was a long, slender boat powered by long oars arranged in rows. The galley usually had only one deck and the side of the ship rose only a little above the waterline.

Egyptians built galleys as early as 3000 B.C. At first the ships were used both as merchant vessels and warships. In later years, they were used exclusively for combat.

Around 700 B.C., the Phoenicians made several changes in the Egyptian galley design. One of their most important changes was the addition of a battering ram on the front of the boat. This device was a timber snout overlayed with bronze or iron, positioned just below the water. In battle, a ship with such a device would attempt to ram an enemy vessel; then the galley's crew attempted to board the enemy craft and overpower it.

Originally, each galley had a single bank (row) of oars. However, in the sixth century B.C., some armies developed galleys called biremes; these had two levels of oars. Within 100 years, the trireme (a vessel with three rows of oars on each side) was constructed; the trireme was the backbone of the Roman fleet during its time of conquest.

Many galleys had a small square sail in addition to the oars. These sails could only be used for cruising when the wind was just right. In bat-

tle, the oars were used almost exclusively.

Although the Egyptians, Phoenicians, Greeks, and Romans relied on galleys, this type of craft was notoriously unseaworthy. It was not designed for prolonged use on the open sea; in rough weather, it sank rather easily. In fact, more vessels were lost in storms than in battles.

The galley continued in at least partial use until the eighteenth century A.D. Before its disappearance, it had been used by many countries in one form or another, having found a place in the navies of Southeast Asia as well as those of the Mediterranean area.

pronged weapon. In the same passage (2 Sam. 5:6-8), there is mention of the "blind and the lame." Hittite records show that the killing of such unfortunates brought the curse of the gods down on the killers. The Jebusites may have posted these helpless people to defend the city, but David ignored the curse and took it anyway.

The wars of David may be divided into two types—those close to home in which Jerusalem served as the center of operations and wars away from the home base. The second type required a base of operations that had good communications with Jerusalem and the front lines. It had to be easily defended. It required a good supply of food, water, and facilities to manufacture and repair weaponry. And it must have a government loyal to David. Mahanaim met all these qualifications, being a center for metal works and having a government especially loyal to David (cf. 2 Sam. 17:27-29).

David's first war with outside nations was against the Aramaean-Ammonite alliance (2 Sam. 10–12). There were three routes from Jerusalem to Rabbah, the capital of Ammon: (1) The first was the shortest and fastest route, but involved a 1,200-meter (1,300-yard) climb inside enemy territory that was exposed to the enemy and difficult to defend. (2) The second was a medium-long route that went through rough, broken territory inside the enemy country and was open to attack by the enemy. (3) The last was the longest route that led through Israelite territory and crossed the Jordan near Samaria, an Israelite stronghold. The army could then resupply at Succoth and be in a position to attack either to the north (Aram) or to the south (Ammon).

The incident in which General Joab was defeated by a surprise attack, being trapped between the Arameans and the Ammonites (cf. 1 Chron. 19:9-13), is best explained by assuming he had taken the shortest route (1). The Aramaean army had marched south and was encamped south of Rabbah at Medeba, where there was a good plain on which to use their chariots and where they would be able to strike Joab's forces from the rear. So Joab had the Ammonite army to his north, which he knew about, and the Aramaeans to the south, about whom he did not know till it was too late. He was able to avoid total disaster by counterattacking aggressively against these combined forces and turning the battle into a draw. The armies then returned to their respective home bases to fight again another time.

David learned from this incident and adjusted his strategy accordingly. He decided to fight against the Aramaeans first, to stop them from helping the Ammonites (2 Sam. 10:19), and then use the northern route (3) to attack Rabbah in Ammon. Yigael Yadin suggests that this long campaign was fought with the regular army as the main fighting force and the militia (conscripts) being held in reserve at Succoth. The ark was sent along on the campaign (cf. 2 Sam. 11:11), and finally Rabbah was taken (2 Sam. 12:26). As the Ammonite capital was about to fall, Joab called for David to join him and take the proper credit for winning the war. The king was to bring the militia with him to take the city (2 Sam. 12:28-29).

As under Saul, David's army consisted of professional soldiers and the militia, or the drafted army. The first was divided into two groups—Israelites and Gentiles, the latter being mercenaries. The Israelite contingent was commanded by Joab and had grown out of the "mighty men" who had followed David before he was king. These were from among the original 400 friends of David, many of them having been dissidents under Saul (1 Sam. 22:1-2). These later grew to 600, with many of them distinguishing themselves in battle and perhaps in individual duels with the enemy (cf. 1 Sam. 23:13; 27:2; 1 Chron. 11–12). When David became king, these men became his royal strategists and advisors and were made the officers of the standing army, responsible for training and commanding the civilian militia. The top men were known as the *three*, with the next level being the *thirty*. The exact function of these two groups is not given in the Bible, but since they were the best warriors in the land, they occupied high positions in the army.

As king, David hired Cherethites and Gittites as his personal bodyguard and placed Benaiah over them (2 Sam. 8:18). From among this group of Gentile mercenaries came the *runners*, the king's special escort corps. They first appeared under Saul (1 Sam. 22:17) and are mentioned during David's time (2 Sam. 15:1); they seem to have been a regular part of the king's retinue. David used this corps of foreigners to settle rebellion within his own family, as for example the war against Absalom (2 Sam. 15:17-21). This practice followed the example of the Egyptian pharaohs, who had provided themselves with men who were loyal only to the king.

The other part of the army was the militia, probably commanded by Amasa (cf. 2 Sam. 20:4-5). Since they were civilians and had home responsibilities, they were difficult to assemble quickly. But the militia was called out to join the army in its struggle against Absalom, and the whole was divided into three units, headed by Joab, his brother Abishai, and Ittai. Amasa had gone over to Absalom and was head of his army (2 Sam. 17:25). After the rebellion was crushed, Amasa returned to David's side and was appointed the commander of the militia (2 Sam. 19:13; 20:4-5), while Joab remained as the commander over the professional army. Later, in another time of crisis, Joab killed Amasa (2 Sam. 20:8-12) either because he doubted his loyalty to David or because of personal ambition. Subsequently Joab was restored to his former position as commander of the entire army (2 Sam. 20:23).

David organized the militia into twelve divisions of 24,000 men each, one division serving on active duty for one month each year. They were trained and readied for battle by the professionals (1 Chron. 27:1-15). Each tribe tended to specialize in the use of particular weapons (cf. 1 Chron. 12), and each of the twelve divisions may have consisted of specialized units from each of the twelve tribes. The central government assigned the number of units each tribe was to supply to the militia, while the local tribal authorities determined which men went on active duty (cf. 1 Chron. 27:16-

Cavalryman. the Aramean cavalryman astride his prancing horse on this basalt relief (*ca.* ninth century B.C.) is armed with a shield and a club or sword. His hair hangs in locks to his shoulders. He is beardless because clean-shaven soldiers could not be seized by the beard in combat.

22). The local authorities could also summon the tribal militia to meet local needs such as policing and emergency raids or withstanding invasions. As much as possible, the tribes supplied their own units.

David's census, for which he was judged by God, was probably a military one in which he sought the age and location of potential draftees for the militia (cf. 2 Sam. 24:2-9; 1 Chron. 21:6; 27:24). Other military censuses are recorded in Scripture (2 Chron. 17:14-18; 25:5; 26:11-13), but the motivation for this one was wrong. It is interesting to note that Joab, the professional soldier, was opposed to this plan of David's, reflecting perhaps the professional's disdain for the draftee.

Another change that came during David's reign was the use of chariots in Israel. In Saul's day the Canaanites fielded 30,000 chariots and 6,000 cavalry against him, but he as the judges before him had no such weapons (see 1 Sam. 13:5). The biblical record does not give us the details, but David began using chariots, probably those captured from the Canaanites (cf. 1 Chron. 18:3-4). When David hamstrung the Aramaean horses instead of capturing them, this may have indicated that he already had sufficient chariots. By this time the Aramaean chariots were manned by two soldiers, and perhaps so were David's.

Under Solomon, chariotry became a major unit in his army, involving many chariots, horses, and extensive housing for them (1 Kings 4:26; 10:26; 2 Chron. 9:25). That he had so huge a force has been verified by Egyptian and Assyrian records of the time; he probably made good use of captured Canaanite chariotry. Having so large a force probably protected him from outside invasions and maintained peace in that part of the Near East. It is interesting to note that many years earlier Samuel had predicted that having a king would involve this expensive equipment, which would then have to be supported by much higher taxes (cf. 1 Sam. 8:11-18).

The extensive use of cavalry units would come at a much later time, but some were used in Israel. As neither saddles nor spurs were used by the troopers, they had less stability and less control over the animal than they needed.

Solomon was especially active in building fortifications (1 Kings 9:17-19; 2 Chron. 8:3-6). We know how Solomon built his fortifications, for archaeological discoveries at Megiddo, Hazor, and Gezer have given us a good picture of what they looked like (cf. 1 Kings 9:15). Solomon simply copied the fortifications of the previous period by using casemated walls, whose outer shell he thickened, and also improved the gates.

D. The Period of the Divided Kingdom. The major military influences of this period were the great Mesopotamian powers of Assyria and Babylon. Warfare continued as before, with no particular changes being made offensively or defensively except in the improvement of existing weaponry. The Assyrians improved their offensive weapons, so their enemies improved their defensive ones, particularly the architecture of their fortifications.

The period opened with warfare between the northern and southern kingdoms (Israel and Judah), as each tried to establish itself as an independent power. At this time, Aram was the major rival in the area and fought against both kingdoms. Assyria was on the rise and would soon be the major influence in Palestine. Although the Bible has little to say about him, Omri of Israel must have been a very capable military leader (885–874 B.C.). Assyrian records speak of his kingdom as the "Land of Omri" a century or so after his reign. Apparently his abilities in war and politics, which included his conquest of Damascus of Aram and his alliance with the Phoenicians, earned him the respect of Assyria. Omri and his son Ahab strengthened the fortifications of Samaria, the capital of the northern kingdom. Although the biblical accounts of warfare in his period are not too detailed, Assyrian monuments and inscriptions provide many detailed descriptions of their activities in the Near East including Palestine.

Assyria's major weapon was the chariot, though the Assyrians also used spearmen, bowmen, slingers, and cavalry well. For their soldiers' defense, they made good use of coats of mail and shields. They were excellent tacticians and were able to transport their troops and equipment over all kinds of terrain. Their tactics included fighting on all kinds of terrain, including amphibious operations.

Assyrian pictorial records show the development of the chariot in great detail. At first this offensive weapon was manned by two men, then by three men by the time of Sargon (722–705 B.C.), and finally by four men by the time of Ashurbanipal (669–633 B.C.).

One Assyrian bas relief shows the capture of the city of Lachish by Sennacherib (704–681 B.C.). It shows a Judean battle chariot, which is like those of Assyria, having a yoke for four horses. The personal chariot of the king had a three-men crew, two soldiers and an armorbearer, on whom the king's life might depend.

Israel, the northern kingdom, was still using chariots at the time of Ahab, for the records of Shalmaneser of Assyria (859–824 B.C.) record that Ahab sent 2,000 chariots and 10,000 infantry, perhaps his professional army, to help him at the Battle of Qarqar. After him Israel's chariot force diminished, till at the time of Jehoahaz (814–798 B.C.) he could only field 10 chariots, 50 horsemen, and 10,000 infantry (cf. 2 Kings 13:7). Israel, and presumably Judah, became more and more dependent on the great powers and entered into an era of "power politics" to insure their survival as nations. This showed their continual lack of trust in the God of Israel in their looking for help in human strength and weaponry, and brought on them the condemnation of the prophets (cf. Isa. 31:1, 3).

The biblical account of the wars between Ahab of Israel and Ben-hadad of Syria (860–841 B.C.) shows how God's people won some of their battles through superior tactics, such as maneuvering their enemy into an indefensible position (see 1 Kings 20). Ben-hadad had besieged Samaria and demanded its surrender (vv. 2-3). The wording of the demand was interpreted to be figurative, so Ahab agreed to submit, expecting only the paying of the usual tribute (v. 4). The Aramaeans, however, wanted to loot Ahab's family, palace, and city, so after consulting with his elders the king of Israel agreed only to pay the tribute rather than surrender to the literal demands of the Aramaean (v. 9). An exchange of threats followed, and Ben-hadad, who had his army camped at Succoth, some miles to the east, set out with an advance force for the capital of Israel (v. 12). Since it took time for armies to march in those days, Ahab was able to muster his militia (v. 15) and lay a trap for the advancing Aramaeans. At noon they attacked the Aramaeans in a narrow valley near Tirzah and thoroughly routed them. They pursued the fleeing Syrians to their camp at Succoth and thoroughly defeated them, for Ben-hadad and his officers, certain of victory by the advance force, had become drunk and were not able to fight (vv. 16-21).

A prophet of God then came and warned Ahab that Ben-hadad would try again in the spring. That season was the favorite time for oriental kings to launch their invasion campaigns, for it allowed their armies to travel in dry weather and put them in enemy territory at harvest time when the farmer-militiamen would be busy in the fields and unprepared for battle. The time would also enable their armies to live off the foodstuffs of the land they were invading. Meanwhile Ben-hadad was told by his advisors that the "gods" of Ahab were mountain gods and that the Aramaean should therefore avoid the mountains and fight on the plains, where his chariots would prove to be superior. Ahab, however, met the Aramaeans at a narrow pass leading to the plains and so defeated a larger and stronger force. Ben-hadad's troops fled to Aphek, which Ahab besieged and captured. Ben-hadad surrendered and begged for mercy. Contrary to God's instructions through the prophet, Ahab let him live and made an alliance with him rather than depending on his greater "ally"—God (vv. 31-34, 42).

Jehoshaphat of Judah (876–848 B.C.) used similar tactics against the Moabites, the Ammonites, and their allies. The enemy was ambushed in one of the Judean canyons and was so completely surrounded and exposed that they surrendered without battle (cf. 2 Chron. 20:16). The kings of Israel and Judah often used their knowledge of the geography of Palestine to fight against and win over their enemies (cf. 2 Kings 6:8-12; 2 Chron. 13:13-14). A notable exception occurred toward the end of this period when Josiah went to battle against Pharaoh Necho (609–593 B.C.) and fought him on the plains near Megiddo instead of setting an ambush in the hill country. Josiah was killed in battle and Judah was defeated. This was a common tactic in ancient times, for to kill the king was to cut off the army's head (see the instructions of Ben-hadad in 1 Kings 22:31).

After the decline of Aram came the rise of Assyria. That nation's superiority in open warfare drove the lesser nations of the Near East to start building better fortifications to withstand Assyrian sieges. The cities of Judah and Israel apparently were successful in doing this, for Assyrians are often pictured as besieging them. The siege of Samaria, for example, took three years, and later God warned Judah against trusting in her fortresses (Jer. 5:17).

The Assyrians, to match their enemies' improved fortresses, developed the battering ram into a more effective weapon, but their enemies built new, thicker non-casemated walls to counter it. One type of Assyrian battering ram had six wheels, a wooden frame, and sides covered with wicker shields or other light material that would prevent spears or arrows from penetrating. These battering rams were approximately 4.5 to 6.5 m. (5 to 7 yd.) long with a 65-cm. (26-in.) base and a domed turret, possibly covered with metal, in which the ram was suspended by a rope and was used like a pendulum. Peepholes in the turret allowed the crew to guide the machine to the right part of the wall and fire arrows at the defenders. The turret was about four yards high and the front of the section housing the ram about a yard high. The head of the ram was like a large metal axe blade, which was driven against stone walls in an attempt to collapse them. The crews of some of the rams included "dowsers," who threw water on the firebrands the defenders threw on the weapon (see Sennacherib's ram, 705–681 B.C.). Tiglath-pileser III (745–727 B.C.), called "Pul" in the Bible (2 Kings

Attack by Assyrian army. This drawing, made from a relief in Sennacherib's palace, depicts the Assyrian army's assault on the city of Lachish (*ca.* eighth century B.C.). The Assyrians attack with bows and arrows and battering rams, while the inhabitants of Lachish throw stones and shoot arrows at their enemies.

15:19; 1 Chron. 5:26), developed a ram that moved on four wheels, had a lighter body than previous rams, and could be more easily dismantled, transported, and reassembled. Sennacherib improved even more on its lightness and ease of assembly. A century or so later, the pictures of Ashurbanipal's reign (669–633 B.C.) show no evidence of the use of rams. He used scaling ladders on enemy walls, because he apparently felt it was a waste of time to transport unwieldly rams around to the cities of the enemy.

The Assyrians also invented and used mobile towers, from which archers could cover the advance of the battering rams by shooting directly at the defenders on the walls. In order to get these weapons close to the walls, the attacking army would often build dirt ramps (cf. Ezek. 42:21-22) topped with rocks or logs to cover the sharp embankment at the lower walls to bring the rams and towers to the walls.

Often several rams would be concentrated on a single point of the wall while attempts to undermine or scale the wall were made at other points. Assyrian pictures of the period show enemy walls being attacked by battering rams, axes, swords, spears, fire, scaling ladders, and undermining at the same time. This forced the defenders to spread their men along the entire wall instead of concentrating at the place where the wall was being dangerously bat-

Siloam Inscription. This six-line inscription is carved into the rock wall of the lower entrance of the Siloam tunnel, south of Jerusalem's temple area. Probably made by a workman, the inscription gives details on construction of the tunnel.

Tunnel of Siloam. This tunnel dates from the reign of Hezekiah (eighth century B.C.), who diverted water from outside springs through the underground passage into Jerusalem's Pool of Siloam. The tunnel is over 500 m. (1,750 ft.) in length.

tered. The attackers were also protected by round and rectangular shields, the latter being of body length and curved at the top. They would protect the men doing the undermining. Supporting infantry was used to help those attacking the wall.

Another tactic employed by a besieging army was to try to cut off all food and water supplies to the enemy city (cf. 2 Kings 6:26-29, where we read of a famine in Samaria when it was besieged by the Syrians). Kings defending their cities tried to stock up and assure adequate food and water supplies if they were expecting a siege. Hezekiah's engineers dug a tunnel through almost 550 m. (600 yd.) of solid rock to give him a water supply (2 Chron. 32:30). The Siloam Inscription (Hebrew writing found on the walls of the tunnel) describes the work, which was begun at opposite ends and joined in the middle. Other fortress cities show evidence of wells, cisterns, complicated drainage systems, and underground tunnels to provide water for the city. The Bible describes Rehoboam's efforts at building fortresses and how he provided supplies for them (2 Chron. 11:6-12). The kings of Israel and Judah studied the construction and defense of cities carefully. We are told that Uzziah (790–739 B.C.) invented "engines" that shot arrows and threw large stones at the besieging enemy (2 Chron. 26:15). Some scholars think these may have been catapults, but Assyrian pictures dating from this period and subsequent times show no evidence of them. Yigael Yadin suggests that these "engines" were special structures built on towers behind which the defenders could stand upright, still be protected, and be able to shoot at the enemy. However, the Lachish picture shows a screen of shields protecting standing defenders.

According to the Bible, Uzziah was the first king who equipped his entire army with helmets and breastplates (2 Chron. 26:14). Previously such equipment had been the possession only of kings and special fighters in Israel (cf. 1 Sam. 17:38; 1 Kings 22:34), though other kings equipped all their troops with them.

Because of the difficulties and great expense of sieges, kings and commanders often tried threats and tricks to get a city to surrender. So it was that Jehoram was not willing to believe that the besieging Aramaeans had left (cf. 2 Kings 7:10-12). Attackers also tried intimidation (cf. 1 Kings 20:1-3) and direct threats. When Sennacherib besieged Hezekiah's Jerusalem, he verbally attacked Judah's army, the Egyptian alles, and God Himself (2 Kings 18:19-23). Hezekiah's representatives in the negotiations asked the Assyrians to stop speaking Hebrew and use Aramaic so the defenders would not be panicked. The answer was that they were using Hebrew as a tactic to do exactly that—lower the morale of the defenders and cause them to revolt against Hezekiah. The soldiers stayed loyal and the siege was resisted. Sennacherib never took Jerusalem (as he did Lachish), but according to his records he "shut Hezekiah up like a bird in a cage."

Babylon finally managed to conquer Judah by taking all her fortresses and besieging and taking Jerusalem. Everything in the land was destroyed and the people taken into captivity, which was another military tactic to prevent the rebellion of captured peoples.

Later, in the restoration, only Jerusalem was rebuilt (by Nehemiah). The land would not see war again till Maccabean times.

E. The Rise of Greece. During the fifth and fourth centuries B.C., the Greek city-states developed volunteer citizen armies to defeat mighty Persia. However, these city-states fell prey to a series of disastrous civil wars and a new power, Macedonia, arose. The Macedonian army copied the close-order battle tactic known as the *phalanx,* which had been developed by a general named Epaminondas.

Philip, king of Macedonia, willed his army and throne to his son, Alexander, under whom Greek military tactics and culture spread throughout the Asian world. Alexander's successors were rulers of what were called the Hellenistic kingdoms.

F. The Military Genius of Rome. The Romans, who fought with the Greeks first in Italy and then in the Greek islands, copied and improved upon their enemy's well-organized military units. They built a truly citizen army and a powerful navy. It was the Romans' talent for building and organizing that brought down almost all their enemies.

One by one, small kingdoms of the eastern Mediterranean fell to Rome. The great visionary text of the Essene collection of the Dead Sea Scrolls, entitled *The War of the Sons of Light with the Sons of Darkness,* describes in detail the last great battle in which the Roman army destroyed the Jewish state in A.D. 70.

FOOTNOTES

Chapter One: "Trade"

[1] James B. Pritchard, Ed., *The Ancient Near East: An Anthology of Texts and Pictures* (Princeton, N.J.: Princeton University Press, 1958), p. 19.
[2] Pritchard, *op cit.*, p. 17.

Chapter Six: "Laws and Statutes"

[1] R.J. Rushdoony, *Institutes of Political Law* (Nutley, N.J.: Craig Press, 1973), p. 53.
[2] Luke plays down Pharisaic debates, while Mark never uses the Greek word *nomos* (law). John's portrayal of Jesus is so unique that it would be confusing to discuss it here.

Chapter Seven: "Warfare and Weapons"

[1] John Murray, *Principles of Conduct* (Grand Rapids, Mich.: William B. Eerdmans Company, 1957), pp. 107-122, 178-180.
[2] *Ibid.*, p. 179.
[3] *Ibid.*
[4] Other authorities believe that verse 8 may simply mean that David's men fought their way up to the spring of Gihon, located just outside the city wall, to cut off the Jebusites. They could have done this without crawling through the shaft.

ACKNOWLEDGMENTS

The Publisher gratefully acknowledges the cooperation of the following sources, whose illustrations appear in this book:

Gaalyah Cornfeld, 71, 76.
Judith Dekel, 153.
Egyptian National Museum, 80, 134.
Elsevier Publishing Projects, 105.
Episcopal Home, Matson Photo Service, 28.
Fototeca Unione, 72.
L. H. Grollenberg, 31.
Harvard Semitic Museum, 98.
Iraq Museum, 138, 142.
Israel Department of Antiquities and Museum, 8, 14, 44, 45, 56, 82, 154, 155.
Israel Government Press Office, 113.
Istanbul Museum, 7.
Jewish Theological Seminary of America, 106.
Levant Photo Service, 63.
The Louvre, 101.
Charles Ludwig, 62.
B. Mazar, 17.
Metropolitan Museum of Art, 78.
Naples Museum, 92.
Oriental Institute, 3, 55, 88, 97, 131.
Palestine Exploration Fund, 9.
Claude Shaeffer-Forrer, 100.
University Museum, 42, 58, 91, 116, 123.
Vatican Museum, 145.
Bryant G. Wood, Word of Truth Productions, 29.
Yigael Yadin, Israel Exploration Society, 137.

The Publisher has attempted to observe the legal requirements with respect to the rights of the suppliers of photographic materials. Nevertheless, those who have claims are invited to apply to the Publisher.

INDEX

This index is designed as a guide to proper names and other significant topics, found in *Public Life In Bible Times*. Page numbers in italics indicate pages where a related illustration or sidebar appears. Headings in italics indicate the title of a book or some other important work of literature. Use the index to find related information in various articles.